# CAN YOUR MARRIAGE BE A FRIENDSHIP?

❖

*Patrick J. McDonald, LSW, BCD*
*and*
*Claudette M. McDonald, LSW, BCD*

Paulist Press
New York/ Mahwah, N.J.

Book design by Jay Gribble, C.S.P.

The Scripture quotations contained herein are from The Jerusalem Bible, copy-
right © 1966 by Doubleday & Company, Inc., and from *The Message: The New
Testament in Contemporary English*, by Eugene Peterson (Colorado Springs:
Navpress Publishing Group, 1993).

Library of Congress Cataloging-in-Publication Data

McDonald, Patrick J., 1939-
    Can your marriage be a friendship? / Patrick J. McDonald and Claudette M.
McDonald.
        p.   cm.
    Includes bibliographical references.
    ISBN 0-8091-3621-X (alk. paper)
    1. Marriage—Religious aspects—Christianity. 2. Friendship—Religious aspects—
Christianity. I. McDonald, Claudette M., 1948-. II. Title.
BV835.M213    1996
248.8´44—dc20                                                    95-26055
                                                                    CIP


Published by Paulist Press
997 Macarthur Blvd.
Mahwah, N.J. 07430

Printed and bound in the
United States of America

# Contents

———◆———

*Dedication*

To all the couples
Living and dead
With whom we have journeyed
Into the mystery of love

———————————— ❖ ————————————

# Introduction

❖

Our gift of healing has matured during the last twenty years, evolving into a deeply shared identity. Consequently, much of our married life has been spent helping other couples find their way to healthier marriages.

Even though we invite the blessing of God upon every aspect of healing, it is achieved through the application of the ordinary techniques of marital therapy: learning to communicate, resolving conflicts, sorting through gender differences, clarifying roles and constructing new expectations for the marriage.

For many couples, however, the external structure of a marriage no longer satisfies. They hunger for a deeper relationship, and this is tied to a desire to approach the God question. Thus they ask for guidance about a marital spirituality. We have written this book in an effort to assist them with this task.

There are a variety of ways to define, examine and implement a marital spirituality, and this book represents just one approach to this largely unexplored topic: the notion of *friendship*. We will use it as a foundation for everything we say, and in doing so we will highlight two significant realities.

First, friendship plays a major role in the survival, development and enrichment of marriage. We often hear couples refer to their marriage as a genuine friendship, then contrast it to romantic love. Romance is seen as short-lived and tenuous but friendship as long-lasting and authentic. For these and other reasons which we will develop in the main body of this book, we assert that underlying every healthy marriage is a healthy friendship.

We have also discovered that for many couples like ourselves, friendship opens out into a deep relationship with God. It becomes the source, foundation and model for a spirituality of marriage. A couple's awareness is that of a God who actively participates in every aspect of their friendship. Thus, our second assertion is that God initiates a friendship with couples and through that friendship invites them into the heart of divine love.

This beautiful reality lies at the heart of the gospel. As a couple comes to terms with what friendship with God means, their friendship with one another is changed, deepened and transformed. The invisible God is made visible in their friendship.

There are a large number of books on the nature of friendship, and this information is easily applied to friendship in marriage. It is the product of good communication and hard work, and we believe that any effort to deepen friendship in a marriage brings with it great benefits to the couple as well as to those around them.

Our orientation for this book, however, is different: we begin our exploration of friendship in the heart of the New Testament. Here, the compassionate God, embodied in the person and life of Jesus, invites us into deep friendship. By this very fact, we are challenged to reflect upon the significance of friendship with one another, for through it we enter into the mystery of God's love. In brief, we become friends with God as we become friends with one another. The application of this profound message to friendship in marriage is easy: it becomes the doorway through which a couple enters into the realm of divine love.

Couples may or may not be fully aware of what is happening to them as their friendships unfold. As we often instruct them, the development of a spirituality is partly a matter of "listening to the voice of God" already at work within the dynamics of a growing friendship. The hard tasks of understanding one another, resolving conflict and deciding what they want from each other are all important. But to hear the voice of God is to open up the friendship to hidden richness as they enter into deep friendship with God at the same time. On the other side of the door awaits a treasure house of gifts that make marriage an unbelievably rich experience.

There also awaits the mystery of divine love (agape) which presses a couple to reach for a selfless love they generally know dimly in their early history. The unfolding of the demands of selfless love and the outpouring of God's limitless gifts work hand in hand; and at the center of this odyssey awaits an encounter with the living God.

If what we say makes sense to you, we invite you

to incorporate the information into your marriage. If you don't agree with what we say, feel free to use the information as a backdrop against which you can define your unique relationship even more clearly. We are the first to agree that there are many ways to look at marriage, and exploring it under the umbrella of friendship is only one way.

In the final analysis, marriage is what a couple makes it, and any positive developmental processes that lead to a richer marriage have their own value. If our book helps you think more creatively about your destiny as a couple, then our time spent writing it has been worthwhile.

# 1

# Foundations for a Spirituality of Friendship

*I call you friends.*
*John 15:15*

———————❖———————

"Hey, P.J. and Claudette, just what do you mean by marital spirituality?" probed another curious member. The pointedness of his question jolted both of us to attention. It surfaced during the meeting of a study group we attend regularly at a local house of prayer. We were in the midst of a discussion of a book on contemporary scripture studies, and the inevitable questions were beginning to develop about how the night's new information would blend into the differing spiritualities represented in the group.

"Like all spiritualities," one of us began, "there are a varieties of ways to look at marital spirituality, but one thing that makes it so different from an individual spirituality is that it is shared by husband and wife. It is in the sharing itself that the spirituality comes to life and matures."

It was obvious that our questioning member was not satisfied with the answer, so he probed a little more persistently, "But you still haven't told us much about a marital spirituality except in a general sense. Give us a definition." There was a brief pause while we looked at each other, searching for the familiar cues for who would answer, since the questions were aimed at both of us. "Friendship," came the answer. "Marital spirituality is nothing more than a reflective friendship." Another pause. Then the information flowed a little more spontaneously as we rallied behind one another, sharing our perspectives and firming up our incipient ideas into solid statements.

"Friendship," we continued, "bonds people together in a lasting way in a marriage. It outlives romance. We find, in the marriages that are alive and healthy, that married couples have developed beautiful friendships, and they grow by simply reflecting on what their friendship means to them. By doing so, they find a rich life. We simply term marital spirituality a reflective friendship."

"But does that make it a spirituality?" someone else objected, her animation visible in the energetic way that she approached her dilemma. "You haven't said anything about God."

"Every couple is different," we answered, still alternating responses with one another as we made an effort to weave together our thoughts into a coherent pattern. "A reflective friendship allows couples to share the sacredness of life in a meaningful way and they feel good about it. Others brush up against the God question as they move into the deep and rich rewards of long-term friendship. Still others savor the love of God in every one of their interactions, and their deepest reflections on friendship are when they pray together. Yet all these couples enjoy a spirituality. They arrive at it from different directions but all share the capacity to creatively reflect on the significance of friendship in their lives."

The discussion worked its way to a final conclusion that night and the study club was brought to a close. Memories of the candidness of the group's questions remained with us for the next several days, helping us both to think a little more creatively about marital spirituality. We continued to be caught up in a deepening curiosity about how the two great dimensions of friendship (human and divine) intertwine with each other and weave their ways into the complex and beautiful tapestry of a marriage, so sacred to couples.

At times we find a clarity in our explorations of marital spirituality and we can say something profound about it. Sometimes we share our frustrations because the differences between the two dimensions of reflective friendship are not easily drawn. Most of the time we simply stand in awe before the great mystery of marriage as we do our best to explore its many layers and themes. In order, then, to explore the significance of both the human and divine dimensions in the development of a marital spirituality, we will begin with a story of long-term friendship.

## The Story of a Friendship

The midwinter darkness settled in gently, bringing with it a light powdery snow which accented the upscale neighborhood in a delicate veneer. "Nice send-off!" someone remarked, as several of us converged on the house at the same moment. The dinner party was composed of several couples like ourselves: all good friends, pleased to be wrapped for one last time in the beautifully decorated home of our hosts. Even though it was late January, the place was filled with reminders of Christmas. Stacked here and there against the walls of each room were shipping boxes of various sizes and shapes, each holding a portion of the family history and awaiting the arrival of the moving van.

The guests chatted away about anything and everything while they sipped their refreshments, resting their cocktail glasses in random fashion upon the nearest shipping box. The disjointed and spontaneous chitchat rolled along undisturbed as we took our places at the dining room table, where the lavish dinner setting seemed comically out of place amid the rooms full of boxes. The room quieted down as we sat. Then someone proposed a toast; so we raised our glasses of chardonnay and joined in. Our host couple sat before us, becoming more misty-eyed the longer they listened to the outpouring of good will directed at them.

"Here's to your future, Patsy and Ken," one of the guests intoned. "We have been through a lot together as friends, as neighbors; our boys have grown up together, so we hate to see you go. But we also wish you the best of luck in your new life and hope that we will always stay connected as friends."

The emotions of the moment began to swell as the gathering of close friends drew deeply from a collective reservoir of pleasant memories. Sentiments flowed as easily as fine wine. Someone quipped, "Remember us all back here when you become rich and famous." The thick intertwining of emotions brought laughter intermingled with sadness overflowing with tears in a series of exchanges that were grippingly telling of long-term friendships.

Then it was time for the host to say something. "You are all such good friends," he said. "We appreciate your friendship and your care for us on this cold winter night." He paused and swallowed, unable to finish. Patsy carried on for him, "Yes, such good friends. We'll miss you, and we invite you all to come to visit us and go skiing and be with us whenever you can break away. We deeply appreciate your friendship and will never forget our time here. Let's stay in touch."

There was another brief pause. The well of smart things to say had apparently run dry. The silence was broken as our wine glasses "clinked" together in a last gentle crescendo of praise to the joy of enduring friendship. Laughter filled the unspoken void, the evening enfolded around us with its gentle warmth, and the meal began. We forgot about the future for the moment.

### Saying Goodbye

Every person has said goodbye to a friend at one time or other, and most people recount that it is never an easy task. This farewell was no different. It deeply touched everyone present, reminding us that life from now on would be a bit more tenuous and a lot more seasoned.

This goodbye came as a reflection of the life of corporate America twenty years ago. Ken had opted for another move, this time seven hundred miles further west. This would be his fifth move in twelve years. The rules for success in his company were surprisingly simple: if you are on the way up, you move; if you want to get to the top, you move often.

Patsy was not terribly pleased with the prospect of disrupting her career as a psychotherapist in midstream, but she made the best of it. Loyalty to her husband outweighed every other value. She hoped she could find a job in the mental health field in Salt Lake City, but would check out the job market after they settled into their new home.

Their two boys were in the middle grades and they seemed to have little trouble with relocating. Their sense of adventure about yet another move was sweetened by the call of the finest powder skiing in the country.

One week after our farewell the movers emptied the house of all belongings while the family set out to construct a new life in Salt Lake City. To those of us who secretly envied their upward mobility, protected and nurtured as they were by corporate America, it looked as if life held out to them limitless possibilities. Indeed, we toasted their good fortune, but we also toasted ourselves that we might be so lucky. In reality, we were lifting our arms in a gesture of resignation to the ambiguously unfolding proposition of life in our mid-thirties, none of us really knowing what was in store. No one could have told us how different it would be twenty years later.

## Night Reflections: Friendship Revisited

This story recounts the love, the attachments as well as some of the difficult questions about change and separation that were so alive for several couples one winter evening. As we toasted one another at this farewell meal, we toasted each other's future; but wrapped within the endearing statements in each of these toasts were all the myths about life and love that are so appropriate for couples in their mid-thirties.

The prevailing myth that gave form and substance to the entire evening was the belief that all present were really in control of their lives. That shared belief made the night resonate with everyone as a deep human experience, filling it with the laughter and joy of lives lived freely and energetically.

As we discovered through the process of living, loving and staying in touch with one another for twenty more years, the full implications of what we wished for one another that night would become apparent only later. The awakening of the great lessons of mid-life and the consolidation of our separate wisdoms would come to fullness during other magic moments as we reflected on the mystery of marriage and the magic of friendship.

## Late Night Encounters

It was night, and Patsy and Ken were back with us for a visit. It was time to sit by the fire, drink a few beers and once again share the meaning of friendship and marriage. It had been twenty years since the gathering of friends had toasted their good fortune at the winter night's farewell banquet.

We had enjoyed regular contact with them as their lives continued to unfold, complete with the manifold perks of success. They moved to new locations on a regular basis, each move representing for them new opportunities. As they evolved into the middle years of life, however, the moves became less adventuresome. They described their last two relocations as, "hopefully, the last one." Early retirement looked very inviting.

Meanwhile, their children finished high school, college, married and joined the family business. Patsy was a high achiever. She developed great competence as a therapist, beat the odds and founded a successful practice in every place they relocated. It was especially difficult for her to leave several practices behind in order to begin anew in another state.

Our life continued to unfold as well, as did the lives of all the friends who gathered that winter night. Our practice grew and flourished as the joy of a healing ministry evolved into our central identity. The memories of the winter farewell dinner had evaporated, lost somewhere in the shadows of life lived twenty years ago.

The first sad news came late at night, the strident ringing of the telephone jolting us into an awareness that something, somewhere, must be wrong. The call was from Patsy's sister, anxiously informing us that Ken had become seriously ill. He had contracted a rare blood disease: a precursor to leukemia, and he might need a bone marrow transplant. When we finally reached Patsy, Ken had already been in the hospital for several weeks, but he was surviving. The outlook remained guarded.

We now sat before the fire once again listening to them complete the story of how Ken's illness had unraveled their dreams of a more grounded life. They talked at the same time about the awakening of a new spirituality.

For two full years they had searched for an appropriate medical treatment to arrest the disease. They traveled to clinics across the United States and Europe, looking for one last miracle cure, but they had found none to date.

Their loyalty to one another had deepened every mile of their journey. They learned to pray jointly. They continued to viscerally explore the full implications of the call to committed love.

They are now are members of a community of believers who join them regularly in heartfelt efforts at prayer. They continue to learn what joys a loyal friendship can offer when life brings a severe test. They place an ever-deepening trust in their friendship that began more than thirty years ago. The feelings of vulnerability remain very strong as they seek a way to arrest the disease. They are constantly reminded of their total dependence upon God.

As we sat by the fire and talked about life this

night, we were all much more cautious about definitively planning for a future. We talked more about our desire to live simply, our comfort with deep surrender and the need for greater trust. There was a fresh willingness to listen for the voice of God in our experiences. There was also the haunting feeling, shared in different stories by each of us, that the real substance of life resided just beyond our capacity to control it.

The intertwining between the known and the unknown in our lives had brought us again to a moment of sharing, but it had also left us with the capacity to say less and surrender more. But all was well that night and our friendship had deepened. The shadows created by the burning fire danced on the wall as we shared our visions and wished each other the best of life and health. Then the shadows lifted their glasses high and drank to one another once again.

## Reflection on Divine Friendship

Our view of marital spirituality as a reflective friendship not only flows from the very human task of growing in friendship, but from a relationship with God. By its very nature, friendship brushes up against sacred realities as couples do the hard work of understanding the full implications of what their friendship means to them. It may or may not bring them into relationship with a personal God, but they often describe their deep experiences of friendship as "sacred" or "a gift" or "a mystery," which in turn points them toward deeper truths. For others, the entry into a reflective friendship is intimately connected to a relationship with a personal God. They see a loving God as the foundation for a shared life as well as the source of their most contagious joys in their daily reflections on what this presence means.

Even though we see great variations in the ways that both the human experience of friendship and the questions about the presence of God are addressed, every thoughtful friendship shares one common theme: the presence of God and the development of friendship are inextricably intertwined. In approaching one dimension of this reality, the other is necessarily addressed.

In order to shed some light upon this matter, we will again reflect upon a story, this time from the heart of the New Testament. We turn to the gospel of John, with his artistic and compelling exploration of the symbols which present us with the mystery of God.

## John's Gospel

"It was just before the Passover feast," notes John in his gospel account. The first sentence of his recounting of the final days of Jesus would culminate in the telling of his death and resurrection. "Jesus knew," he continues, "that the time had come to leave this world and go to the Father. Having loved his dear companions, he continued to love them right to the end." (Jn 13:1)

The previous week in Jerusalem had been a conflictual one. The growing tension between Jesus and the religious authorities had placed the entire community on edge. Fear and suspicion governed the relationships even among his closest disciples. An uneasy peace existed. There had been rumors of double-dealing, even betrayal within the inner circle. This closely-knit group was quite confused about what was happening to them. A thousand questions remained concerning their final destiny.

As late afternoon shadows lengthened into the beginning of the great feast of the Passover, Jerusalem quieted down. Families sequestered themselves in their private rooms for the celebration of the Passover meal; uniting them in solidarity with ancient ancestors who had escaped from Egypt under the protection of their saving God. The night claimed a mood of story telling and journeying to a better life in the promised land.

John captures the mood of Passover time by playing with shades of light and darkness in his narrative. "It was suppertime," he simply notes. He also heightens the drama of these last days by darkening the character of Judas, "The devil by now had Judas, son of Simon the Iscariot, firmly in his grip, all set for the betrayal." (Jn 13:27)

Like all good Jews at festival time, Jesus and his family of followers retreated to the upper room for the Passover meal. The atmosphere was charged with tension and suspiciousness as the ancient ritual began to unfold. But in spite of the tension, suspiciousness and complications of the interaction among the friends who had gathered, John's account presents a picture of close friends who gathered together for a meal.

In simple terms, John portrays the God of light and life who loves his followers so much that he extends the rich gift of hospitality to them through the sharing of a meal. As with any gathering of friends for the last time, the deep reflections on the meaning of their friendship, the shared thoughts about life in the now and in the future, dominate their sharing. The rich symbolism of the sharing of a meal bonds them together in a most intimate way. The time of the Passover was especially significant for this group, with its deep historical reflections on the passing over for all of them from death to life.

John notes that it was night as Judas left the room in the middle of the meal to initiate his act of betrayal. He also notes that the tension was so high, the specter of betrayal so real, that Jesus became "visibly upset" by the events of the evening. He realized that his hour of emptying-out was drawing near.

With the mood of the Passover darkened by troubled conflicts among his closest friends, Jesus began to express to them the guidelines for those who would call themselves disciples. It offers a profound reflection on the deeper implications of friendship itself.

"I've loved you the way my Father has loved me," he disclosed.

> Make yourselves at home in my love.
> If you keep my commands you'll remain
> intimately at home in my love.
> That's what I've done—
> kept my Father's commands
> and made myself at home in his love.

It is easy to imagine the reactions of those present: reaching hard to comprehend the simple yet

demanding laws which would govern the relationships
of those who are to follow. He continued:

> I've told you these things for a purpose:
> that my joy might be your joy,
> and your joy wholly mature.
> This is my command:
> Love one another the way I have loved you.
> This is the very best way to love.
> Put your life on the line for your friends.
> You are my friends when you do the things I
>     command you.
> I am no longer calling you servants
> because servants don't understand
> what their master is thinking and planning.
> No, I've named you friends because I've let you in
> on everything I've heard from the Father.
> You didn't choose me, remember; I chose you,
> and put you in the world to bear fruit,
> fruit that won't spoil.
> As fruit bearers, whatever you ask from the Father
> in relation to me, he gives you.
> But remember the root command:
> Love one another.
>
> (Jn 15:12ff)

## Friendship with God

Although the New Testament account of the love
of Jesus for his friends might seem like an unusual
place to expand our explorations of a spirituality of
friendship in marriage, we suggest there is no better

place to do so. It is here that we can begin to develop some thoughts on the divine dimensions of friendship.

The gospel brings us into contact with a God who invites us into friendship, and the invitation comes through the rich symbol of hospitality (a room prepared and a meal shared) initiated by God. John presents this ritual of the bonding of friends as more than just a moment in history for a select few disciples. He presents it as a universal call to anyone who hungers to listen to the voice of God. It reaches down through the centuries to include a vast multitude of people who have accepted the invitation to open up their lives to love: individuals, couples, saints, sinners, professional religious, the marginalized, the poor and a great blend of people, both living and dead. It is an invitation to all humanity to come to the table of the Passover feast to be nurtured into a life of love and service by a gracious God.

For married couples, to listen to the voice of God in their midst is to share life, love and bread and to know that God dwells within this sharing. The choosing of a meal to speak definitively about God's love for each of us places every meal, every experience of a shared life within a sacred context. The rich symbolism of this meal tells us that God literally toasts our efforts at life and love and thereby becomes an intimate part of the sharing.

The specific kind of love Jesus reflects upon with his friends is translated in the Greek New Testament as agape. That is a much deeper and more difficult kind of love than philia: the simple love of friendship. Both Greek words are used in the New Testament to describe the nature of friendship, but philia represents a generous kind of love that is more like the love and loyalty associated with a family or a clan. Jesus is speaking of more than just a simple sharing of values that binds people together in a clan or family-like movement of discipleship, brotherhood or sisterhood.

Agape expresses the highest ideal of Christian love. It asks for nothing in return. It implies a complete giving of the self simply because the person loves freely and without reservation. It is an image of the love of God who loves unconditionally. The highest expression of agape in the life of Jesus is seen in the crucifixion. It became the ultimate and final statement of how much God loves us. "No person," Jesus reminds us, "can have greater love than to lay down one's life for a friend."

The term agape carries a similarly special significance for anyone who accepts the call to be a follower of Jesus. Very simply stated, God loves us with an unconditional love, and because of this pure gift we are asked in turn to reach for the ideal of unconditional love in our relationships. Thus, in marriage, the richest gift as well as the most provocative challenge is to work toward this ideal of agape.

To love well means to love selflessly. To mature in love is to undergo deep changes in a transition from early romantic love to genuine selflessness. Embracing the ideal of agapic love is to identify with the heart of Jesus. It implies more than just identifying oneself with the family of believers. It brings with it such a strong identification with the ideal of selfless love that it implies a daily crucifixion of our own.

Loving in this way is an open invitation for husband and wife to journey together into the heart of God. It is to be immersed in the deepest mystery of their existence. But an immersion in mystery does not make it an easy journey. Sam Keen, a modern student of the mystery of life and relationships, speaks poetically of the very human and very difficult task of selfless love:

> The alchemy of an unconditional love that heals us only takes place when a man and a woman, knowing the best and the worst of each other, finally accept what is unacceptable in the other, burn their bridges, and close off their escape routes.[1]

## The Blending of Human and Divine Love

John's gospel, then, not only allows us to see into the inner life of God but it also sheds light on the nature of human friendship. The application of these realities to marriage is simple and straightforward. When a couple see themselves as friends of God, this cannot help but texture every effort they make at being good friends. Every gesture of friendship brings with it an opening into the domain of God's own love. As their friendship matures in wisdom and freedom, they enter into the fuller implications of this mystery. If they live out the invitation to reach for agape, their entire friendship is transformed through the presence of God. God becomes an intimate part of their friendship because they come to know the intimate God who dwells with them. A reflective friendship in this sense moves a couple into the inner life of God.

This places friendship on a much higher plane than the simple joy of sharing life with one another. The hard work of cultivating, nurturing and maturing in friendship is still demanded, but the very act of becoming more intimate friends immerses the couple in the mystery of divine love.

Like a colorful summer sunrise, framed in the sensual smells of a passing shower, the image of the invisible God becomes clearer to couples as they reflect on the full implications of what their friendship means.

## What Does It All Mean?

"What do you mean by a marital spirituality?" couples continue to ask. When we describe it as a "reflective friendship" it makes a lot of sense to them. The phrase comfortably resonates with their own experiences of sharing life, love and bread. They are reminded of their own pleasant evenings by the fire, recounting to one another what it means to be such deep and loving friends. Their hard work of making a more satisfactory marriage dissolves in these moments into a shared awareness that beneath all the uncertainty lives the gracious God who feeds their souls and invites them into deep wisdom.

"Is a spirituality for everyone?" couples sometimes ask, doubting that the rich gifts we describe could be available for them. "Yes," we repeat boldly. "God's gifts

are open to everyone who wants them." Then we usually add, "The beginning of any marital spirituality is
sparked by an awakening to the gifts that are already
at work within your lives. Discovering them is where
the first reflection begins."

# 2

# Awakenings

*Make yourselves at home in my love.*
*John 15:9*

---❖---

## The First Awakening: Romance

There is a taste of the sacred in every love, a joy of homecoming in each embrace; for lovers never really tire of recounting to one another the pleasure and the pain of their relationship. We describe these captivating moments between lovers as their first awakening to the call of love.

Every awakening has a magic about it. Some describe it as a mystery: the excitement, the deep emotional charges lift a couple onto a different plane of existence. It is the first glimpse of the turquoise sea under the warming sun. Love redeems. It changes one for the better, and the first awakening brings with it songs, wine, poetry and the undiluted joy of just being together.

In the early stages of romance, there is little worry about which experiences will last and which will fade. The magnetism of the now is what counts: we are together, we are a couple, we exist!

"We were really romantic at first," she related. "We just sort of knew this was it for each of us. We knew that the future would unfold somehow, so we didn't get too formal about where we were going with this relationship. We just shared and lived, enjoying each other's company as though we only had each other. We never really reflected on it as a great friendship. That just seemed to take care of itself. It was as though this is where we each belonged, and we accepted it because it felt so right."

Like this couple, the powerful swells of romantic love speak to lovers about who they really are. They are carried along by its magic and mystery and seem not to worry about more lasting matters. For the fortunate ones, friendship awakens in its due time.

## The First Awakening: Friendship

In contrast to those couples who place a strong emphasis on romance, we find many others who discover one another through a different celebration of homecoming. They embrace a deeply shared solidarity in the redeeming qualities of friendship.

"There was no doubt for me from the beginning that this love was something special," she said. She was recounting their earliest days together, trying to reconstruct the components of the special magic that first brought them together. "The lights just sort of went on and I found a clarity that was wonderful. I had dated a lot and knew that I wanted someone who would be loyal and loving to me, and this guy just seemed to fit. It was very special from the beginning. I think it was trust that really began it all. We never had reasons to mistrust each other; it just seemed to be there."

As she reflected upon all that had taken shape for them during their twenty years of marriage, she consistently referred back to the attribute of trust. It was clear that this was the primary bonding quality in their lives together. "We relied more on that sense of trust to keep us together than anything else. We never really talked about it as such; it just seemed to be there, sustaining us when we needed it. Its value is clearer now, and we appreciate it even more."

This couple's awakening began as a tentative friendship grounded upon trust and a belief in its enduring value. For the next twenty years they explored the implications of their first embrace and worked hard to develop the fullness that their early trust implied.

Not every love awakens, however, under the unblinking eye of trust. For some, their first embrace is around the qualities of friendship that form the bedrock for what will mature later: honesty, openness, caring, compassion and other shared values. The blending of deeply shared visions is usually described as a "completion" of their developing personhood.

"I never really found much of a grounding for my life," she repeated several times. It was clear that she was trying to capture the significance that her relationship with John had brought her. "I had been through a number of relationships, some of them very destructive and very empty. I wondered if I was ever going to find someone I could really care about. But when I first met John, there was no rapid heartbeat, no excitement, no real emotional kick, but there was an awareness that he was the one."

She smiled as she arrived at her truth, her voice growing stronger as the full conviction that "he was right for her" became more apparent. "I had this awareness that something missing had been found, as if there was a completion or a connection that gave me something I had been looking for. John and I started talking that afternoon and we haven't stopped since."

Couples like this seem to know from their first exchanges that their deepest bond is in friendship. Some are adolescent or even younger when they meet, but even then they could name the qualities of the friendship they embraced and still find great comfort in sharing them with one another after many years of marriage. Their awakening to love is usually practical, balanced and reflective.

"I think the most attractive part of that early experience was the capacity to talk to her," he disclosed in a matter-of-fact way. He shared his story with a fresh innocence and visible pride. "She was just sort of there for me, and I felt myself talking easily and comfortably in ways that I had never talked before."

He was clear about the fact that he and his wife felt comfortable with one another from their first long conversation together. "I couldn't believe I really talked that way. We just shared for three hours, and they wanted to close the place up, but we just kept talking.

They finally began stacking chairs around our table and we got the hint. I guess I discovered something that night that was totally new to me. I could talk about myself, and the more I talked, the closer I felt to her. I'll never forget how beautiful it was."

## The Discovery of the Hidden Self

Safely ensconced within the security provided by the comfort of shared values, the hidden self begins to emerge: a new confidence, a discovery of latent talent, an energy, an excitement for life and hope for the future. It blossoms as the magic of love captivates and its mystery deepens. This can be surprisingly new for a couple even if it marks an awakening from a deep sleep that descended as a previous marriage failed.

"I had been through one marriage and it was terrible, mostly because we married far too young. Neither one of us knew what we wanted, so we blamed each other for making life so miserable."

Her narrative was an admittedly difficult one. As she talked, she felt the feelings of shame and guilt re-emerging that she thought had died with the divorce. She fought back her tears and continued talking anyway: "A year later, we were divorced and I started back to college, really skeptical that love held any promises. My skepticism lasted for another five years, but I did get through college and ended up with a pretty good job with a marketing firm. By this time, I was defending my fragile little self very well, able to take men and their boring lines with a grain of salt."

She quickened the pace of her story, looking

much brighter as she related her good news. "When Jeff and I talked it was different. I couldn't believe he didn't want something. I had to work very hard to keep control over my doubts and my old skepticism. But as we talked, and I talked a lot for the first time in several years, I felt something coming back to life in me. I fought it at first because I didn't want to get hurt again. There was a trust there I had never experienced and it felt right. We have been together five years now, and I am just a different person."

As this young woman discovered, the emergence of her new self was coaxed to life through the interaction with someone she could deeply trust. Her new self was described as the opening up of a fresh appreciation of life itself. Sometimes, however, the emergence of a new self is viewed as a coming back home to a number of fundamental values that were lost when an early relationship failed.

Awakenings vary immensely in their evolution, content and style. They can come to life within the context of a stand-alone friendship or they initiate an entry into a relationship with God.

### A Spiritual Awakening

The first hints of God's presence in the life of a couple can be as simple as a shared sunrise or as archetypal as the discovery of a destiny in the stars. Some of them seem to carry with them an awareness that they are joined by a deep spiritual connection from their very first days together.

"When I first met Jack we were students at St.

Mary's grade school together. It just seems that we were friends from the very beginning. We would walk home from school together, talk about what was going on in class and just be friends to one another."

Her story was a beautiful one as she reflected upon their sixty years of friendship. "We stayed friends all during high school," she continued. "We dated other people, but always came back to our friendship with one another. We were clear about sharing a love of God and somehow knew that God had brought us together. That has never really changed. We have been good friends for sixty years and have shared a common love of God in everything we do. More and more we see God's love in everything."

Every statement reinforced their deep beliefs in the central place of friendship for their marriage. It was equated with being at home in God's love. It opened up their lives to deep love. It sustained them through the long years of career development and child-rearing. It still sustains them as they face the most difficult crisis of their life together: serious health problems.

Jack spoke for the marriage this time, "I have a degenerative eye disease, and I am now legally blind. Sue helps me get around, writes for me, reads to me, and has been so patient with my impatience. We are still each other's best friend and have been that way since grade school."

## Glimpses of the Hidden God

This couple presents a rare picture of those who began their relationship with solid friendship based upon a conviction of the importance of a spirituality. They have blended the two together into a synthesis of comfort, loyalty, trust and caring that has given their friendship deep roots and their relationship with God enormous depth. They are unshakable in their loyalty to one another as well as their calling to plumb the depths of the mystery of God in their lives. Agape now invites them to enter into a level of spirituality they have never known before.

For the majority of couples, however, the deep connection between their own friendship and a friendship with God is not so clearly defined. Their spirituality awakens with the first touch of the sacred: a kiss, a feeling, an experience of their sexuality or a vision of how profound a shared life really is. That often prompts them to want to know more about a spirituality and what implications it carries for their lives.

"We were pretty immature when we first met," she stated. She had an opportunity to reflect upon how their relationship had matured, so she welcomed the opportunity to talk about their evolution. "There was a lot of intensity and romance; now I realize that we were both needy at the time. We sort of devoured each other since we were both so hungry for approval. Somehow, though, we came to see that the friendship with each other had a lot more substance to it than we first imagined. We could always talk, so we brought out our concerns and found our way through them. The caring and loyalty that was often lost in the distraction of romance brought us back to one another. They lasted through some very hurt feelings. We have emerged through these early days with a very deep friendship.

Every so often, I get a sense of how good it really is—there is a sense of awe about it, maybe even having to do with God."

## Sorting Out: Romance and Friendship

The awakening of a couple's spirituality, no matter what year it begins to quicken, usually takes form through the interplay of romantic feelings and the shared affirmation of a genuine friendship. Both have their unique place in this awakening. Romance keeps their spirit alive, renews them with charges of interpersonal electricity and sustains them with much-needed energy.

Friendship reminds them of fidelity during difficult times, gives them support when needed, a trust when the world is threatening. Friendship remains during periods of emptiness and boredom and is not easily destabilized by the rich array of feelings that come and go in a marriage, especially during the early years.

Sorting out what is real and what isn't about romance and friendship can be painful and difficult. It brings with it moments of profound ecstasy as well as moments of complete emptiness. During some of the empty times, it can be difficult to see anything sacred about the marriage. Only the stubborn belief that they do have a destiny together and the conscious return to the genuine qualities of friendship keep some couples together.

Deep in the intricacies of their interaction the process of sorting out goes on: experience by experience, awareness after awareness as they make an effort to determine what will last and what is transient. The elation of romance melts into the awakening of deeply-held truths about what really holds them together.

"We knew we could be good friends from the beginning," she revealed, "but we really got stormy with one another at times." She laughed quietly and became pensive as she tried to describe her arrival at their truth. "We knew we were moving along toward something more serious, but I think we were both afraid of what a serious commitment implied. Now I know that the fighting over hurt feelings was just another way to sidestep the hard questions about what friendship means and what the implications were for our future."

Her manner changed again and she smiled as she revealed her special story, "I thought about our deep friendship and all the hard work that led up to this moment. We were flying back from Cancun. He was listening to music on the headset. He took them off and placed them over my ears. Someone was singing, 'you are my lover and my best friend.' He looked at me as I listened to the music, kissed my cheek ever so tenderly and squeezed my hand. My heart nearly burst. I knew he was my best friend and this was what really held us together."

## A Coming Back Home

As couples describe for us their awakening to the deeper realities of friendship, they often describe it as a homecoming. The storms associated with the sorting out process have diminished. They are aware that some of their early dreams have died in the disappointment of unmet romantic needs. Yet they still return to the relationship as the familiar place in life they have carved out for themselves. They arrive at a realization that what holds them together is of greater significance than romance, more stable than their dreams. The rediscovery of deep friendship confirms them in a comfort, confidence and loyalty to one another. They believe they have traveled full circle to their own place of origin.

"It seems as if I have always known him, for my whole life," she reiterated. She was describing for us the return to the grounding in the marriage that she found so stabilizing for herself. Her description referred time and again to the feeling of a coming home.

"Even before I can remember—I guess from the moment I first talked to him—there was a desire to spend the rest of my life with him. He gets on my nerves when we are around each other too much. When we are away from one another, I miss him. When we come back together it is wonderful. I try to enjoy every moment that we have together, because I know his illness has given us limited days. We really are best friends, and we know it."

Coming back home to the relationship does not mean that the revolution takes place easily or naturally. It often implies a long struggle to sort out what the friendship means, communicate with one another, prioritize basic values, understand some real differences between men and women and do the hard work of building upon the initial awakening that first brought them together.

## "How Do We Develop a Spirituality of Marriage?"

We hear this question time and again from those couples who desire to move beyond their first awakening into the developmental phases of a marital spirituality. "Where do we begin?" they ask with all sincerity. "Do we learn to pray or do we remain practical and work hard to become better friends?" They challenge us to be clear about what we mean by a marital spirituality, then explain how to develop it from its beginning stages through a rich fulfillment.

"Very simply," we suggest, "the best place to begin is to stay loyal to the experience of friendship as you know it and respond to the full implications of what that call means."

"Start where you are," we instruct, "and reflect on your lives together in order to understand and appreciate what your gifts are. Then awaken your friendship to new possibilities." We suggest to them that by deepening their relationship and working together to move it to a more mature level, they can begin to taste the joys of a shared spirituality.

We explain that the call to friendship they feel in their marriage can easily be interpreted as the voice of God. The best way to respond to this voice for now is to work to deepen their friendship with one another. By its very nature, this will move them closer to the sacred. We then offer some very practical advice about how to proceed. In brief, we describe these exercises as efforts to move more deliberately into the joys of a reflective friendship.

We observe that they are usually somewhere within three modes of developing, and we suggest the following beginning options for creative reflection.

### Option 1: Improving an Already Existing Friendship

This option assumes that a friendship already exists between husband and wife and they are in accord that a solid friendship is very important. They also hunger for an awakening into something deeper. The steps are as follows:

1. Do an inventory with your spouse and begin to become aware of the many gifts that exist in your marriage (example: your life, your children, your achievements, your friends and family). Reflect on any or all of these gifts and then decide what qualities in your friendship have brought you to this moment in your history together (example: support, generosity, hard work, resourcefulness, trust, honesty, etc.).
2. Discuss which of these qualities you want to prioritize and which you want to de-emphasize. Are there any other qualities you want to add to those you are already confident about?
3. Now jointly decide how you are going to reprioritize them in a practical way for the next thirty days. Set some goals for yourselves about the ways that you will implement these tasks. Agree to discuss your progress on a weekly basis.
4. Take an evening and find a quiet hideaway and just be with each other. Share a meal. Take the time to talk and discuss: What was your new effort at building friendship like? Did you live up

to your own goals or did you fall short? Try to arrive at an awareness of where the successes and failures came from. Now restructure your next set of goals.

## Option 2: Creating a Friendship That Does Not Exist

This option is for those who would like to begin a spirituality of friendship, but have never taken any deliberate steps to construct it. These reflections can help you move from a beginning desire for closeness to a genuine implementation.

1. Find some alone time and think of three qualities of friendship that you most deeply value. You can use the examples of friendship that come from your background. Perhaps you remember a "best friend" who embodied these values and who taught you about how life-enhancing they are. Write down the three qualities and reflect on some ways that you desire them to become a part of your marriage. Be very specific about how these might be brought into the marriage.

2. Now find a private space where you and your spouse can really be present to one another. You might try sharing over a meal in your favorite place, perhaps one that you associate with your early romance. One person at a time, read to your spouse what you have written. Be sure to read your reflection very slowly to make sure you have been heard. Then trade assignments. Make sure you have each been suffi-

ciently heard in order to help each other reflect upon what friendship can mean to each of you.

3. Now do some discussing of what you have each written. Decide on the quality you would most like to implement in your beginning marital friendship. Discuss some ways you can begin to make this quality more practical. Set some concrete goals and then agree to meet weekly in this very place and talk to one another about how well or how poorly you are progressing toward genuine friendship.

## Option 3: Coming Back Home to Friendship Following a Transition

This option is for those who have experienced the collapse of their romantic love. Perhaps the collapse has left an aftermath of emptiness and discouragement, prompting the belief that there is nothing left in your marriage.

These exercises can help you reflect upon and discover some deeper qualities that provide a foundation for continued growth in friendship. They might even provide a reason to stay in the marriage.

1. Take an evening together and be alone—really alone, without phone, friends, distractions. Make sure you have plenty of time to talk. Three hours is recommended. Now talk to one another about the disappointments you have experienced as your romantic love has declined. What differences do you now see in one another that you did not anticipate? Share the empty feelings that have resulted

from the collapse of the feelings in your marriage. Take plenty of time to make sure that you are being honest, non-blaming and open with one another.

2. Now talk in general terms about what friendship means to you. What are the fond memories you hold about having a best friend? How did you know this person was a best friend? How did you communicate as best friends? How did your relationship with this best friend grow? What lasting gift did this friendship leave you with?

3. Now share what qualities of friendship you find in your marriage that echo these experiences. What stories can you tell about where you have discovered friendship hidden under romantic feelings? Were there any elements of friendship that gave form and substance to your romance with one another? Are any of these elements left? Do you desire to begin a friendship with one another as a new awakening for your marriage? Decide where you want to begin. Set some goals for yourself related to what you have discovered and agree to meet again in one week to measure how you have implemented these goals.

We realize that every couple is different, and the stories of how changes unfold in a marriage vary immensely. If the reflections we have suggested above do not relate to your situation, try one or all of the following.

## Alternative Options

a. Do an inventory on yourselves: Have you retained any of the qualities of friendship in your marriage that were there from your early days? Do you want to reclaim any of them and come back home to the marriage? If so, which ones do you want to reclaim? Decide.

b. What qualities of friendship do you most long for that you learned from earlier friendships with someone special? What one would you like to incorporate into your marriage? Ask your partner if he or she would be willing to form a friendship around some of these qualities? What qualities is your spouse asking for in return? Now decide what two qualities you are going to begin to implement in your marriage. Get practical and decide how you are going to put these new efforts at being friends into practice.

c. What *listening* to one another do you still need to do in order to get rid of the anger that comes from being disappointed about the loss of romantic love? Let each other know. Then try to forgive one another for the disappointment. Now begin thinking about the fact that good friends can forgive one another. Talk honestly about life. Work hard to hear each other. Discuss: is this enough for you to begin to be friends again?

The development of a viable spirituality of friendship offers its unique gifts and challenges at any time during a marital history. The impact of gender questions, role expectations and what marriage itself implies touches every couple in some way or other. The picture is further complicated by the fact that conflicts about gender and their influence upon roles in a marriage are often undergirded and activated by unresolved dependency needs, emotional immaturity and unrealistic expectations for the marriage.

Even the question of what friendship *means* to a man and woman can vary dramatically, making the task of building a friendship a complex one. If the friendship is to mature and the differences are to be incorporated into a genuine spirituality, gender questions must be reflected upon by both partners. We consider the reflection upon these differences so important that it demands specific treatment. We will address the men first about these matters, then the women.

# 3

# For the Men:
# Views About Women

❖

As we established previously, the foundation for
the New Testament ideal of love is grounded in the
Greek word agape. It invites you to make continued
efforts to break out of your narrow views of self and
work to understand the reality of the other. Thus,
agape calls you to reflect upon and ultimately deal with
the significance of some very real differences in the
ways that men and women view friendship. These differences create vastly different expectations for what a
friendship brings, and unless they are taken into
account, a marital spirituality can collapse.

Even the most earnest prayers offered in the spirit
of agape will not exempt you from the hard work of
understanding what these differences mean. God's
generous love builds upon a couple's hard work. It is
presumptuous to think you can sidestep some real differences while at the same time asking God to ensure
that your love lasts.

Expectations within the same-sex friendship often

seem easier and clearer: the men have their fishing trips and the women enjoy their leisurely lunches and face-to-face sharing. A friendship between a man and a woman, however, demands special consideration, for it can be loaded with political and interpersonal implications that can either test it to the limit or bring a couple the genuine richness that flows from the magic of appreciating gender differences.

If you want to be your wife's best friend, then it is important that you understand what friendship means to a woman. To proceed on any other basis is to treat your woman friend in a casual way and run the risk that you will lose her friendship through misunderstanding, boredom or conflict.

## Noting Some Differences

Much has been written recently about the differences between men and women and how these differences are influenced by the great social, political and economic changes in today's world. If a solid friendship is to underlie a marriage and open it up to the potential richness that a deeply shared life holds, these differences must be taken into account.

We have heard a number of thoughtful people recently despair that men and women could ever find a stable accord in friendship. They see the differences between the sexes as so divisive that men and women appear to come from different planets. John Gray, a couple therapist and popular author, makes that very case as he describes some of the deep differences in the ways that men and women view relationships:

The most frequently expressed complaint women have about men is that men don't listen....The most frequently expressed complaint men have about women is that women are always trying to change them....No matter how much he resists her help, she persists—waiting for an opportunity to help him or tell him what to do. She thinks she's nurturing him, while he feels he's being controlled. Instead, he wants her acceptance. [2]

Gray descriptively expresses some of the real difficulties with men and women understanding one another, but at least acknowledges that it is possible to achieve an understanding. Others are so immersed in the ongoing gender wars that they declare the state of affairs between the sexes hopelessly grim and endlessly hostile. There is no alternative left except to fight for separate territory and thereby keep it inviolable.

In our work with couples, however, we have discovered that there are, indeed, genuine differences between husband and wife. Their discovery often comes with surprises, tears and disappointments. But for those who pursue a mature friendship, the differences can meld into shared strengths that bring great joy to the marriage.

Jay and Erin were excited about the forthcoming celebration of their fifth wedding anniversary. Jay had been working on becoming more spontaneous, so he decided that it was time to express his deep appreciation for Erin's love and loyalty during the last five years. He surprised her over breakfast one cold December morning with tickets for the two of them for a love-boat cruise on the western Caribbean. Erin was surprised and pleased and easily shared Jay's contagious joy about the cruise. They parted for their usual day's work that morning with a warm kiss and a shared electricity of anticipation about the winter adventure that lay ahead.

For weeks, Jay talked enthusiastically about the trip while Erin searched diligently for the right baby sitter—one who would live-in for the entire week while they cruised carefree and secure in their five year love.

The baby-sitting arrangements fell together, the time of the departure was at hand, and one brief day later the two lovers were cruising between sun-drenched islands with lush palm forests and white sand beaches. All seemed right with the world and each other, and they felt very close and loving.

However, the second day out of port the weather changed. Strong winds, twelve foot seas, and a love boat that pitched and rolled incessantly brought with them seasickness, misery and edginess to the happy travelers. The captain apologized for the rough seas but said he couldn't do anything about them. He promised to slow down the boat, amend the cruise schedule and find calmer cruising.

Erin discovered that as the week continued to unfold with its litany of bad weather, turbulent ride, impatient passengers and weak appetites, she was angry. In fact, she was livid, and she let Jay know it. The tension culminated with a spirited declaration the last day of the trip that she would have been happier with a bargain night movie and a pizza, and then head home to be close to little Jason.

Jay was crushed, because his newly-discovered spontaneity had prompted him to try so hard to make this event the dream trip he and Erin had often talked about. When he asked Erin why she didn't speak up in December about not liking cruises, she declared, "I didn't want to disappoint you because you were so excited about the trip."

After they arrived safely back home and found an opportunity to process what had happened to them, they each came to appreciate one another a little more. Erin began to understand more about the adventuresome side of Jay and promised him that she would try harder to seek a few exciting options with him. Jay began to realize that Erin placed a higher value on talking, sharing, closeness and being together as a family. Expensive, exotic adventures were simply not a priority for her.

Episodes like this, which sound all too familiar to most married couples, demonstrate just how difficult it can be for men and women to work out the terms of a friendship. However, they can also initiate an entry into the difficult demands of the ideal of agape that most couples would just as soon avoid.

Sometimes the most sincere efforts to reach out and be sensitive, caring and loving can end in misunderstanding, hurt and conflict. At the base of some of the misunderstanding lies the fundamental problem of language.

## Speaking Different Languages

A woman and a man might use an identical word to describe an event or an experience from their intimate life together, yet each have in mind two entirely different realities. Hence, deepening a friendship may very well turn out to be a stormy sea of misinterpretation, hesitancy and alienation until the meaning of a specific word, its context or its significance for each of them is clarified.

When we ask couples, for example, to describe the most important qualities of their friendship with one another, they frequently name *support*. Even though both the men and the women use the same word to describe an important quality of relating, we discover some significantly different interpretations of its use, not only from couple to couple but even within the same marriage.

Some of the men equate support with a practical acknowledgment and recognition of their capability in technical areas. As one husband stated, "Support means making decisions and not worrying about 'I told you so.'"

Support for the women is more often described as "taking time to talk, talk and talk. We are each other's sounding boards. We talk all the time. It is not necessarily a conscious 'nurturing,' we just enjoy talking with each other—sharing, consulting, etc." Thus, the same word *support* often describes different realities for men and women.

They seem to know that support evolves through a process of talking and sharing. But when the men talk about the value of their talk, they lean toward problem-solving. They deeply appreciate their wife's attention to their creativity, personal competence and loyalty to the practical side of the marriage.

When the women talk about support they usually refer to an opportunity to "connect" as persons. Support is often equated with being "present" to one another, sharing life in genuine and deeply-experienced ways and feeling close through the sharing itself. This leads to deeper intimacy.

What we often observe in their different views of support was reflected upon at greater length by Deborah Tannen, a professor of linguistics at Georgetown University. She noted some fundamentally different orientations between men and women that showed up in their language and styles of interaction:

> Though all humans need both intimacy and independence, women tend to focus on the first and men on the second. It is if their lifeblood ran in different directions.[3]

Every husband can profit from learning the same lessons that Jay learned about what friendship means for his wife. But, unlike Jay, there are simpler ways to learn about differences than to be tossed about for five days on an angry sea. The efforts of every couple to come to a common consensus about what friendship means may seem like a voyage upon a turbulent sea at times, but the rewards for trying to do so are great. To understand some basic differences is to set sail upon calm seas under sunny skies and gentle trade winds.

## Calling a Cease Fire

We want to invite you as a couple to call a cease fire to the gender wars for a time. Enough accusations have been made, enough anger expressed, enough of the differences between men and women exaggerated, and enough blood has been spilled. It is now time to appreciate the fact that the very differences that divide the sexes can also offer great richness to a marriage, and the richness can flow if you treat your marriage partner like a best friend. We often refer to this attitude as an effort to build the foundation for a more mature love. We see it as an application of the ideal of agape that Jesus calls us to.

We have discovered in the vital friendships we observe, that husband and wife have not only learned to respect each other's real differences, they have also learned to blend them into strengths. This gives character to the marriage. By encouraging a cease fire to the prolonged and futile gender wars, our hope is that some very real differences are not minimized but simply weighed with cooler heads and more placid emotions.

The risk inherent in our efforts to say something about how men and women differ is that all generalizations about them tend to be limited, or even inaccurate. They simply do not apply to every person in the same way. However, we are willing to take the risks implied in generalizing if it prompts you to reach out to your beloved in more sensitive and caring ways. This will invite you to be a more compassionate person, touch his or her heart deeply and thereby improve the quality of your marriage.

"I think the best part of friendship is the ability just to be myself at times; to share everything about me, to be open and even outrageous in the way that I express myself," she stated. She was describing the simple joy of knowing that she could be her honest and real self and still feel loved by her husband. "I feel free to be myself because his deep acceptance gives me permission to be myself." It was very clear from her comments that this couple had learned to allow each other to be, without pulling one another into needless and endless conflict about their differentness. We identify this capacity as a mark of genuine friendship.

## Connections

Friendship expresses a central value for a woman: she desires to feel secure within herself while at the same time be deeply connected to the man she loves. Unless she feels that the relationship is alive and well between herself and her husband, she is unlikely to feel much vitality about the marriage or even about life in general.

One woman expressed her position in this way, "When we are connected, all goes well with my world. But when we are at odds...one of those days when no matter what we do, we just can't quite get it together, the rest of my day is awful. I can't concentrate on anything."

This example highlights a genuine reality we often observe in women: they place the highest value in their lives upon their special friendships. For a happily married woman, friendship with her husband is the most special. She feels best, functions best and is most alive in every respect when she is meaningfully relating to the man in her life.

Some modern commentators point to this as one of the most essential differences between men and women. They affirm that women place relationships in the most important position in their lives, while the men treat them more casually.

Other reflective critics simply deny that, claiming that a woman's deep allegiance to relationships is just another expression of emotional dependency and they find that abhorrent.

We often observe, however, that for many married women, all values, all judgments, all efforts to infuse life with meaning are measured first and foremost by how their relationships are affected—especially marriage. We also find that other relationship questions affect the ways that women relate to their husbands as well.

Men need to know that women place a high value on the relationships in their life and often cannot be at peace in their marriage while other relationships are strained or conflicted. An example will help clarify what we mean.

Charles decided that it was time to deepen his relationship with his wife Emily. He thought about his options and planned a breakaway vacation for the two of them at an exclusive resort where they could live the carefree life for a week. The trip had been planned for months. They both eagerly anticipated a pleasant time just being with each other, free from the pressures of their demanding separate careers.

Just before departing for their trip, Emily became

concerned about a disagreement she was having with one of her friends. She met several times with this long-time friend to try to resolve their differences, but was not able to achieve the kind of closure she had desired before the vacation trip began. Emily was clearly affected by the misunderstanding between herself and her friend, brooding over it for the entire trip.

Charles tried to do everything he could think of to help Emily enjoy herself, but nothing seemed to work. By the time they were ready to return home, he was irritated with her. He told her repeatedly, "Hey, forget about that disagreement; we're here to have a good time. Let go of it and get into the trip." But she didn't. She couldn't. Her unhappiness clouded the entire trip and their dream vacation ended in tension and discomfort for both of them. It was only when they arrived back home that Emily's personal tension was resolved through a reconciliation with her friend.

No matter what Charles might have insisted about "letting go and having fun," his impatience points toward a reality for many women: they have a very difficult time feeling comfortable with themselves until they feel good about their relationships. Charles would have done his wife a great favor if, rather than nudging her to "get into the trip," he had invited her to share her pain and uncertainty about what was going on in her life. Emily would have felt better about his support, the sharing might have bonded them together at a deeper level, and she probably would have had a more relaxing vacation.

If you want to be a good friend to your wife, affirm her freedom to relate to the significant people in her life as she chooses, and she will feel freer to relate to you. Pressures like "get it together and have a good time" mean little. An invitation to her to share her pain over an unresolved relationship question means a great deal. She will deeply appreciate the fact that you care about her feelings.

### Valuing the Process

Husbands also need to know that their wives will respond more positively to the invitation to friendship if it relates somehow to what we call *process*.

*Process* is a term that is often used to measure the development of a relationship from its beginning stages to a level of rich maturity. Couples sometimes use the same term to examine and understand the sometimes easy, sometimes strained ways that a relationship unfolds as it progresses through the weeks, months and years of its life.

There is a beautiful dynamic enclosed within process as two friends reflect upon what their friendship means to them, how it can be improved, what pleases or displeases them and where they see the friendship going. Process usually unfolds in its most rewarding form through talk, talk, talk. In today's terms, we often speak of the need to process, process, process. One husband summarized process in his marriage in this way, "First we talk, then we golf. Then we play cards. Then we listen to music and have more talk." Perhaps another example will help you understand what process is all about.

Tom desired to deepen his relationship with his

wife. He was aware that Jane had often requested that they "do more activities together," since she felt so isolated at times. He took the cue and invited her to go biking one glorious autumn afternoon.

The colors of the autumn landscape, however, were significantly dimmed for Jane by the time their cycling outing was finished. In fact, she was in tears, and when Tom questioned her about what the tears were all about, she confessed that she now felt more isolated from him than ever.

When they arrived back home and had the opportunity to process what had happened, Tom found out that he had missed the point. He treated Jane as if she biked in the same mode as his competitive male friends: the longer the trip the more valuable the experience. When she explained to Tom that she wanted to bike with him primarily to enjoy his company and only secondarily to add up miles, he was surprised. But he learned. The next time they biked, he geared down his intensity enough to carry on a good conversation with Jane. This time they both felt good when it was over, their feelings buoyed up by a process that spoke to both of them. It allowed them to deepen their friendship through shared activities while they talked and processed and talked some more.

This illustration points out a simple fact of life for husbands: efforts at friendship would be more fruitful if they placed the focus upon both the activity and the process. Indeed, women enjoy activities that are creative and fun, but they also respond beautifully to processing what the activity means for growing into a deeper friendship. Talking, sharing and measuring the meaning of their experience with their beloved are all close to the heart of a woman. This is often in contrast to the men who can be overly-focused on goals, accomplishments and end results.

Deborah Tannen reflects upon the different ways that men and women view process and how this affects their ability to understand one another:

> If they do have heart to heart talks, the meaning of those talks may be opposite for men and women. To many women, the relationship is working as long as they can talk things out. To many men, the relationship isn't working out if they have to keep working it over. If she keeps trying to get talks going to save the relationship, and he keeps trying to avoid them because he sees them as weakening it, then each one's efforts to preserve the relationship appear to the other as reckless endangerment.[4]

## Feeling Good About Friendship

Husbands can also benefit from an understanding that women place a significant value on the emotional dimension of relating. By this we mean that most women feel engaged, spirited, energized and grounded when a relationship is alive for them and they *feel* their experiences at a deep level. Women often disclose to us that they feel most alive when they are actively involved in a dynamic, emotionally-enlivened process of interaction that speaks to them about a growing friendship. We also hear many complaints from them that their husbands remain detached and indifferent during some very intimate exchanges. The women confess that they suffer greatly from this.

Looking at women's orientation in this way is not to recycle the old stereotype that women are more emotional than men, but to simply underscore the fact that women feel quite positive about exploring all the complex and pleasant implications of their interaction with friends. This, of course, includes their husbands.

Sarah kept trying to get John's attention. She kept telling him that she "simply needed to talk from time to time." John was always busy with practical matters and was reluctant to take time from his schedule in order to give her a hearing. Even during their conversations, John would appear to be restless, and then declare his readiness to move on to more important things. One evening as they were talking, Sarah became very emotional, broke into tears, and told John that he'd better begin listening to her or she was going to re-evaluate her desire to stay in the marriage. She disclosed that she felt terribly empty and isolated because he always seemed too busy to listen to her.

John became very concerned for the first time in their twelve year marriage, actually fearing the very emotions that Sarah had opened up with him. But he finally "got it" that he needed to listen. The more he listened, the more she became peaceful and calm, and then talked beautifully about how she saw life, herself and her marriage.

Sarah was so relieved to know she had been heard that she embraced John and tearfully acknowledged to him that she was dramatically different from him, and probably always would be. She *needed* to talk. She admitted that she must talk or feel as if she is "going crazy inside."

Their awakening exchange brought out John's sentiments as well. He acknowledged that even though he tended to be much more self-contained, he was open at last to listening to Sarah. He soon came to realize how important talking was to her. He began to try harder and actually learned what it means to be a good listener. He also learned that Sarah was serious when she said that she needed to talk on a regular basis in order to keep herself emotionally balanced. This sharing for her expressed the most genuine experience of what it means to have a best friend, because she felt it so deeply.

You can bridge the gap with your wife rather easily if you minimize the practical and maximize the listening and sharing. We frequently tell couples, "There is no better way to be best friends than to take the time to really hear one another."

### Face-to-Face Conversation

We often note that women thrive on face-to-face conversation. For many of them, the more dynamic the eye contact, the more valuable the experience.

When we ask couples what helps them feel closest during their efforts at friendship, the women generally focus upon face-to-face conversation. They feel most loved, most appreciated and affirmed when they are invited into their husband's lives for a face-to-face encounter and their eye contact signals to them that their husband's presence is real. For many of them, the more involving the interaction, the more valued the exchange.

As a male you will probably have to do some work to bridge the gap in this area as well, since men generally seem to be less comfortable in this face-to-face mode.

In an effort to shed some light on the intricacies of the communication process between men and women, Deborah Tannen examined in depth a series of videotapes of conversations between the sexes, beginning with young boys and girls and continuing through their early adult years. She made the observation that women tend to be much more comfortable during conversations in which direct eye contact is sustained. The men, on the other hand, are much less secure with it. Many appeared to be visibly uncomfortable, frequently changing their communication postures, then shifting their chairs to an angle to minimize the intensity of the exchanges. She reflected upon the influence of this for later life:

> In all their complexity, these videotapes show that from the earliest ages through adulthood, boys and girls create different worlds, which men and women go on living in. It is no surprise that women and men who are trying to do things right in relationships with each other so often find their partners wanting, and themselves criticized. We try to talk to each other honestly, but it seems at times that we

are speaking different languages—or at least different genderlects.[5]

Her serious studies on the complex layers of interaction in human communication help us understand what we often observe in our own work with couples. The women are very comfortable; indeed, they welcome eye contact as a sign that the men are "in the process." The men often have a very difficult time sustaining any eye contact at all, creating great uncertainty in their spouses who view their behavior as "detached," "indifferent," or even "hostile."

Aaron Kipnis and Elizabeth Herron, a husband and wife team specializing in training programs related to gender issues, also shed some light upon the occluded area of eye contact between men and women and how it relates to closure or conflict in relating.

Women may interpret a man looking away during conversation as being rude when, in fact, it may actually mean that he is feeling relaxed in the relationship, and men may interpret a woman's intense gaze as seductive when she is merely being attentive to the conversation. A smile and extended eye contact from a woman may mean: "I'm dropping my handkerchief and I hope you'll pick it up," i.e., "I'm sexually interested in you." Or it may say, "I'm paying attention to what you're saying/doing and simply being polite, friendly, and cordial," or "I'm intimidated by the power dynamics of our relationship and am displaying soothing signals to you so that you will not fire/threaten/abuse me." How's a man to know?[6]

Amanda and George had been at odds with one another for a number of months. She felt shut out of George's life. She half-believed his story that he was pre-occupied with stresses in his life. George tried hard but never seemed able to break through his discomfort with talking, so their efforts were generally rewarded with lit-tle success. The impasse remained and deepened.

One afternoon, George was called into his boss' office and told that he would probably be without a job in six months due to company downsizing. He calmed his panicky feelings, swallowed hard, immediately phoned Amanda and asked her to be with him this night. He let her know that he wanted to discuss some very important matters with her. They hired a baby-sit-ter, found their way to a quiet retreat and talked into the evening.

George was more honest about himself than he had been in years. He told Amanda that he needed her very much. He also informed her that he hungered for her support and that he wanted to examine the whole fabric of their lives together as his uncertain job situa-tion unfolded. His sincere requests brought with them a pleasant eye contact with Amanda, in dramatic contrast to their interpersonal atmosphere of the past ten years.

Amanda was deeply touched and very responsive. She told George that this was the first time she had felt this close to him in years. This face-to-face awakening to honesty renewed them both, and Amanda felt the magnetism that comes only from the sense of presence that direct eye contact and real emotions bring.

## Attachment and Connectedness

Husbands need to understand that for the most part their wives primarily define themselves as persons by and through their relationship with others, and that includes their husbands. This is often in contrast to the ways that men define their own persons: as a reflection of their goals and dreams for success.

Attachment, connectedness and meaningful interaction with significant others are very close to the heart of a woman. The sheer joy of being deeply connected with a spouse-friend energizes many women as no other experience does. They define their own self in relationship to these very significant experiences.

One woman summarized her position in this way: "I know I can survive in this economic climate. I actually have the earning capacity to do very well, even better than my husband. But I find my deepest satisfaction and my most intimate connection with life when we are together and sharing what it means to be close and loving. This is more than just economic survival. This is what gives my life meaning."

## A Healthy Self

When a relationship goes well, when a woman feels strong and confident, her real self grows and blossoms. She learns to see herself as loving and capable, knowing that the processes unfolding deep within her continue to lead her to self-confidence and personal resourcefulness. She begins to take pride and find strength in her ability to make her own decisions, achieve her personal goals and build intimate and mature relationships. Over a period of time, the strong qualities of selfhood deepen and she learns to express the beautiful and intricate depths of her maturing self. The rewards of a deep loyalty to her personal values and beliefs can often outweigh a husband's detachment, criticism or control. She is no longer controlled solely by what he believes and says.

So central is the allegiance to a formed self for this wife that she spoke confidently about her person in this way: "Marriage starts with the self and ends with the self. We must be responsible for ourselves, 'our stuff,' first by working through our own issues. It also reflects in the marriage. What we are externally, we must create internally first."

We continue to assert: underlying every healthy marriage is a healthy friendship. Underlying every healthy friendship are two healthy selves. In brief, this means that both affirm their separate and distinct "I-ness" and it stays distinct even during their most animated exchanges. Because they each know who they are, they have the capacity to listen to each other, appreciate one another's differences, assert their ideas, values and goals, and then see them as strengths that form the foundation for a lasting marriage. This kind of comfortable give-and-take undergirds any true friendship. In this simple statement, a wife encapsulated thirty-two years of sorting out, defining and working on the terms of a genuine relationship: "Friendship is being so confident in the love of the other person that I am free to act and plan to become the person I want to be."

We find that in the healthy couples, not only is there a respect for each other's persons, but their friendship itself is looked upon as the very source of their most significant growth. This is true for both the men and the women.

Sorting out the tenuous and fluid feelings of romance from the demands of a deepening friendship is never easy for a couple. The struggle to hang on to an emerging self can be difficult, as the ebb and flow between conflicting loyalties to self and other color daily life.

"I find it paradoxical, but absolutely true," she said with the kind of deep satisfaction that settles in after a long struggle, "that we wouldn't be the friends we are today without the fights we had then. Fighting requires intense 'engagement' with one's opponent—it takes emotional energy that I, for one, would not waste on someone I didn't care for deeply. I have seen women who have not fought for their own autonomy with the result that they lost the friendship part of the husband/wife relationship. When we battled, we had to keep before us the principle that if one loses, we both lose."

She continued talking, unfolding a virtual digest of the lessons learned over the years about what it means to be good friends. "Friends don't defeat each other, even when they disagree. We have come to learn that friendship in our marriage requires that we invest in each other's well-being as well as our own. It is a fine line between compromise and martyrdom, but we emphasize compromise if we are to maintain our friendship."

## The Threat of De-Selfing

For many women, however, the development of the mature self easily degrades with stress, then implodes into a black hole of uncertainty and despair. *De-selfing* for a married woman can mean denial of her personal integrity, her principles, values and goals simply for the sake of gaining her husband's approval. Her distinct "I-ness" dissolves in the face of threats of abandonment, disapproval, rejection and criticism.

Her desire to be close, the hunger to please the man in her life, the deep willingness to be intimately connected with her husband can give you enormous power over her. She deeply desires to please you and to do whatever she can to make you happy. The fragile construction of her self can create a situation in which you have the capacity to assist her to become more whole or to disassemble every ounce of self-respect she has worked so hard to achieve.

Frank and Emma have been married for twenty years. Even though they have their ups and downs, their marriage is quite satisfactory for both of them. They enjoy a variety of rich experiences. A circle of close friends and many material comforts have brought with them great feelings of success.

Frank, however, has a temper, and his temper flares when they deal with money issues. Emma is so fearful of Frank's reactions that she won't tell him how much money she spends. Under his intense scrutiny about finances, the fragile structure of her self evaporates as easily as morning fog under the warm noonday sun. She promises again and again to work hard for a more responsible fiscal policy in their household and then actually feels good about her renewed commitment.

But several weeks after their serious money talk, Frank discovers hidden purchases on the charge cards and promptly becomes outraged. Emma de-selfs again by becoming remorseful and hurt, asking for Frank's forgiveness once again. They end the evening at odds with one another, each feeling deeply betrayed and hurt.

De-selfing is not only demoralizing for a woman, it also creates a terrible imbalance for a husband because it gives him far too much power in the marriage. It can easily lead to abuse. As a husband you have a choice. You can manipulate your best friend on the basis of a fragile self or you can learn to be more sensitive and caring about her struggles to be more responsible for herself and the marriage. In a true friendship, agape invites friends to understand the needs of the other person and balance them out with one's own needs.

In this illustration, Frank could not only find their financial situation more balanced, he could help construct a deeper loyalty within the marriage by taking the time to help Emma deepen her confidence in herself. He needs to learn to listen, while Emma needs to learn to be more responsible. This would offer them both a beginning balance for a much healthier marriage.

The struggle to achieve this balance was summarized in this statement by a wife of twenty-nine years. "I think many of the things that made our friendship grow and mature are the very things that could have destroyed it. There has been growth and maturity, but I'm sure it came about in bumps and starts—haphazardly and accidentally at times, all-consuming at other times."

## Inclusiveness

Men need to realize that women are oriented toward an inclusiveness in their relationships. They feel very uncomfortable if someone is neglected, abandoned or hurt. Likewise, they feel quite positive as they reach out to be sensitive and thoughtful to those around them. They generally make a sincere and honest effort to take into account the feelings, attitudes and desires of the important people in their lives. This is especially prominent in ethical questions, where the decision about right conduct may leave one party or another treated unjustly or insensitively.

The magnetic pull toward inclusiveness is especially strong in family life, where a wife can feel terribly pained and empty if family members are not included in a loving circle. Allow us to offer an example of what we mean.

Glenn was determined that he wanted to be close to Amy, his twenty-two year old bride. He was so determined, in fact, that he was quite possessive. He also refused to examine his strong attachment to her which masked his own dependency needs. Every time Amy talked about wanting to be close to her family, Glenn would ignore it, and then schedule a play, a project, a trip or an evening out so that he could be with her exclusively. He labored under the belief that she was responding very positively to his invitations and that they were becoming fast friends.

Amy was haunted by a recurring dream that she was drowning. She would wake up with a start, then lie awake observing Glenn sleeping peacefully next to her, appearing to have no stresses at all in his life. It took her a long time to understand how she could feel such angry feelings for him while at the same time love the person who cared so totally for her.

One night as they sat and talked, Amy began crying and couldn't stop. Taking a very deep breath, she finally confessed to Glenn how badly she felt about missing a family reunion that had been very important to her. She also confessed that she had betrayed herself again by keeping the deeper desires of her heart quiet in order to keep Glenn happy.

After Amy had shared her sad feelings, Glenn in turn claimed that he was deeply disappointed that the evening had been ruined for him. He had his heart set on a good time with Amy all to himself.

They both remained silent and sullen for the rest of the night. Several days later when they talked again, Glenn finally accepted the fact that she needed time to tend to her other family relationships.

To his surprise he discovered that he could be a good friend to her by paying more attention to her needs to include her own family in her life. She in turn was much more responsive to him because now she felt more free to be herself.

## Interiority

Men need to understand that the inner landscape of a woman is familiar territory to her. From their earliest years, women learn to be in tune with and to talk openly about their experiences. This makes them much more comfortable accepting feelings as a genuine part of their lived experience. They likewise learn to feel very comfortable with the internal processes associated with personal growth, spirituality and any endeavor that nurtures life.

We also find that these are the very areas where men register the most discomfort, believing that conversation about internal matters is really a conversation about nothing at all. Men tend to flee these encounters in favor of talking about more concrete matters. Their wives feel hurt and empty, believing that the man whom they desire to be their best friend will not join them for conversation that is reserved for only their closest companion.

Joe and Samantha were not able to talk very easily about deep, emotional matters. Joe felt uncomfortable and registered it in his facial expression, restlessness and edginess, often prompting Samantha to "get on with the conversation." Samantha simply did not understand his impatience and seeming insensitivity. She felt empty and hurt. She also believed that he didn't care enough about her to listen. She wanted so much to have Joe appreciate that center of her person no one else knew. Finally, she erupted into anger one night during some very intense lovemaking, asking Joe in great agony, "How can you desire to be close to me and not want to hear my innermost feelings? I can't handle it any longer."

Joe was seriously shaken by her anguished question. After a night of sleeping in separate beds, he finally began to understand that if he and Samantha were to enjoy a deep and lasting friendship, he needed to learn to be open to the sharing of deeper feelings. He finally began to listen.

## Staying Connected

The joy of working in harmony with others while staying connected to an energizing community is central to a woman's well-being. Therefore, it is unrealistic for a husband to expect his wife to be his best friend if the friendship leads her away from the important connections that are so vital to her.

Mark learned this lesson the hard way. He and Kathy had been married for three years and they were deeply in love with one another. They considered themselves to be each other's best friends. Mark was quite happy with the arrangement and felt he lacked nothing for his emotional life, since he found great joy in Kathy's company.

Kathy confided to him one evening that she was deeply unhappy with her life because she felt alienated from other people. Mark was hurt, believing he had failed in his marriage. Kathy assured him that he had done nothing wrong but that he needed to know a lot more about her. She insisted there was "much more to her" than just being his wife and feeling content with that position.

After a long evening of sharing, they agreed that they were very different in their needs for other people. Kathy affirmed her desire to break out of some of the constraints she felt in the marriage and to be more creative with some new relationships.

She expanded her circle of friends, joined a study group, took a class at the community college, met new friends and even invited Mark to join her in some of her new endeavors. Several months later she announced to him that the new experiences finally gave her the connectedness she needed in order to feel even closer to him.

Mark never did understand what she was talking about, but didn't argue with her conclusions. He simply felt better about the renewal of their shared lives. She still refers to him as her best friend, but knows that she cannot allow herself to slip back into the narrowness which she felt was so debilitating.

## Suggestions for the Men

If you want to find the foundation for developing a deep, genuine and lasting friendship with your spouse, invite her to talk to you about her life. Take some extra time and listen to her feelings. She wants nothing more than to consider you to be her best friend, but knows that she cannot feel close to you unless she feels your deep caring at this level.

Deep in the heart of every woman is the desire to be heard and understood by the man in her life. It is not enough for her to know that your hearing is a polite acknowledgment of the facts and formulas of life. That simply is not enough to hold her in a friendship with you. Nothing helps her feel more grounded, more loved and valued than to have you spend time with her as you listen to the deep desires of her heart. This is a function of a reflective friendship at its very best.

Even though this does not necessarily come easily to a man, it nevertheless implies that if you want your friendship with your wife to deepen and mature, you have to learn to be a good listener. The most difficult task that many males struggle with in the efforts to embody the ideal of agape in their lives is to be a good listener. Yet it is a critical task.

The feelings, issues, desires, inner experiences, and everything that allows a woman to feel close to her own experiences are enhanced and deepened by processing it with the man whom she loves. This is a simple reality to describe, but often one of the most difficult aspects of friendship for men to understand.

Teri and Ray had been through some outrageously stormy exchanges lately. No matter how hard they tried, they could not find a peaceful accord with one another. Their exchanges were becoming increasingly more strained; then Teri would "lose it" and accuse Ray of being insensitive to her needs.

Finally, in an explosive exchange late one night, Ray confronted her with the question, "Why do you save all that emotional business for me? You never let your other friends see this side of you. Am I so special that you have a crazy need to jump on me and unload all your frustrations?"

Teri broke the tension by crying again, answering his question with deep sobs: "You see the entirety of me because I feel free enough with you to be myself when I'm around you. You are the most important person in my life, so you see the real me. I am not close enough to anyone else to dare act this way."

They embraced each other and awakened to a deeper realization that this capacity to share with such intensity was a genuine trust. Ray further broke the tension by asking in a lighthearted manner, "How come I'm so lucky to have the whole package?" The exchange cut through the layers of misunderstanding for both of them. They began laughing and saw the humor in their situation. Ray also began to take Teri's feelings much more seriously. This allowed her in turn to feel affirmed and appreciated.

When a husband desires to be his wife's closest friend, time spent listening to her feelings and validating them as legitimate and real is the cement that bonds a couple together at a deep, caring level. Although the practicalities of life, the urgency to live life efficiently and the desire to fix things can make this a difficult art for a male to learn, nevertheless the rewards are well worth the extra effort.

A woman desires *time* to be with her best friend. Quality time together while enjoying the simple pleasures of sharing is one of the richest treasures in her marriage.

John genuinely desired to be closer to Janet, his wife of eleven years. He believed the way to achieve it was to buy her expensive gifts and invite her to travel to exotic places with him. She never refused the offer, but still felt that the rarified atmosphere of these experiences did not give her the closeness she desired. The tightly programed schedule on these high-priced junkets often left them exhausted, with no time left for sharing what their experiences meant to them.

Janet recalls feeling very empty, parked in a dusty four wheel drive vehicle at the summit of some of the highest terrain in North America. Even an unobstructed view of a solar eclipse from that elevation could not dissipate the shadows of sadness she felt. Underneath her smiles and carefree manner was a deep desire to be elsewhere, in order to find peace with herself. She had to fight back her tears as John kept asking, "Does it ever get any better than this?"

Back home, John extended an invitation to her for another exotic weekend, filled with exciting activities, but this time she declined the invitation. He was miffed by her refusal, since she had always accepted his offers for a new adventure. Rather than concede again when he pushed for her participation, Janet invited him to "quiet down and just be with each other." She made the case that she would feel much better about him if their time was free of the distractions of so many people and so much pressure to *do* things.

Once he got the message, John was quite happy to know that this shift in emphasis would save him $2,500, which he could apply to his next all-male adventure. He began to understand that Janet was just as happy with slow time and quiet conversation. He also began to understand that she felt closer to him when he gave her the opportunity to "feel" closer. They actually reached a mutually acceptable compromise, because John kept his exotic adventure schedule intact. He also slowed down and found a more acceptable way to relate to Janet's needs.

## Reflections: Melding Differences
## into a Spirituality

Again we come back to the question that couples ask so often: "How do we develop a spirituality of friendship in marriage?" In response, we refer again to the notion of marital spirituality as a reflective friendship. Each one of the following exercises can enhance your capacity to creatively reflect on your life together as well as bridge some of the real gaps between the two of you.

Take one or two of the practical suggestions listed below, write them in your date minder calendar, and then twice a week reach out to surprise your wife with your spontaneity, generosity and concern for her.

We believe that any efforts you make to bridge the differences in men and women will be rewarded with a renewed friendship. If a gesture doesn't work the way you imagined it would, don't let a small disappointment destroy your desires to learn more about relating. Try another option in another day or so. The call of agape invites you to try to love selflessly, a matter that can be difficult when your efforts go unrewarded.

1. Imagine that your wife is really your best friend. Invite her to spend time with you twice each week in order to deepen your friendship. Ask her what she would like to do with the time and then honor her request.

2. Practice the simple yet very difficult art of listening to your spouse. Invite her to share her feelings about what happened to her during the course of her day. Listen to her and affirm how

good it is to hear what she is saying. Tell her how much you appreciate her sharing of feelings with you and validate them.

3. Inform your wife that you want her to be more and more your best friend. Ask her what friendship means to her. Share with her what it means to you. Decide on one way that you can express your care for her on this day.

4. Explore with her the whole notion of connectedness and what it means for her. Ask her how you could be supportive to her in her struggles to bring richness to her life in some of these matters.

5. Ask your wife to share with you what you communicate to her about your ability to converse with her in a face-to-face dialogue. Decide how you are going to be more patient with increased eye contact. Ask her to listen to you as you explain to her how difficult it is to communicate in this fashion. Ask her to be supportive as you learn to be more comfortable with it.

6. Reach out to her by writing down all the ways that your friendship with your wife is important to you. Share your thoughts with her, asking her to read them carefully, then try to understand how you feel.

7. Ask her to write out all that your friendship means to her, pointing out to you where she would like to grow closer.

8. Take the word *spirituality* and discuss with your spouse how that word relates to your ideas of friendship. Does it have any meaning

at all for one or both of you? What specific qualities of friendship offers you the foundation for a spirituality of marriage? In what ways might you become more reflective together?

9. Give her the option to go anywhere with you for a weekend breakaway. Ask her where she wants to go, what activities she wants to share and what level of being close to one another she wants.

10. Buy her a small gift just for the sake of doing it. Keep the value of the gift under $20 and work hard to find the best and most appropriate gift you can find for that amount of money. Make the gift say something special about your friendship. Then present it to her while you spend some quality time alone with her.

# 4

# For the Women: Views About Men

◆

If a woman desires that her husband become her best friend, then she too will be challenged to understand the ways of friendship that are more characteristically male. However, in attempting to set out the characteristics that divide men from women, we again run the risk of over-generalizing. As we stated in the last chapter, however, even if we are not accurate in every respect and you begin to relate to your husband with renewed sensitivity, you cannot help but touch his heart.

We do find that men can be very practical about their lives: for example, wishing to "fix things" in their marriages rather than taking the time to listen to their spouse's feelings. Some men, in fact, seem so intent upon fixing things that they are often accused by their wives of lacking compassion and caring.

For every one of these practical males, however, we discover other men who are just as sensitive, just as caring and inclusive in their relationships as their feminine counterparts. They have learned to balance out the call of their own independence with a deep sensitivity to their best friend. At the risk of again over-simplifying, we want to offer some ideas to women about what makes the men in their lives unique, perhaps even different. We also want to suggest some ways to view these differences as beneficial for bridging the gender gap.

## Understanding the Male Species

Little boys learn to be men through a lifelong series of complex learning experiences that point them toward an ever-maturing independence. From their earliest years, they are coached to be self-sufficient, self-determining and autonomous in their efforts to deal with the challenges of life. Consequently, men tend to be more oriented toward independent modes of existence than are women. This, of course, is going to be influential in the ways that they think about, structure and maintain friendships.

These early learning experiences prompt some observers of the male-female scene to make a case for the fact that men form friendships that are based more on shared projects, goals and accomplishments than the creative give-and-take of interpersonal life.

Given the fact that men are taught to be more independent, we can assert that they experience the inner workings of friendship differently than women. They often claim that they have a more difficult time than women in sharing what friendship "feels" like.

Many of them confess that they have to work very hard to express how a friendship is resonating with them.

Once again, as we look for ways to cool down the intensity of the current gender wars, we suggest that women can benefit greatly from understanding one simple principle: *the man in your life is not going to feel the same way you feel.* Nor should he be expected to. He is going to feel in ways that are comfortable and rewarding for him as a male. An example of what we mean will help.

Martha deeply desired to feel closer to her husband. She used to dream about how good it would be if they could just be more comfortable with one another. She knew in the depths of her soul that Ralph, her husband, had great feeling and sincerely longed to have him express it. In order to help him become more involved in their shared life, she encouraged him to speak up more, be more "open" and more aware of the feeling aspects of their interaction. Her honest and sincere efforts to get Ralph to "open up" prompted her to bring him to a marriage encounter weekend, several couple's communication workshops, then finally to professional marital therapy.

Several years, many laborious sessions and thousands of dollars later, Ralph was a bit more open about himself. He had learned to talk about his feelings somewhat more comfortably, he could interact a little more freely, but Martha still felt empty. She placed the blame for her emptiness squarely on Ralph, telling him that if he just talked more she would feel so much better.

The tension grew to ever-higher levels in the marriage. Finally one evening, Ralph opened up to her with the most candid expression of feelings Martha ever remembered hearing from him. He informed her with deep conviction and quivering lower lip that "I am not going to feel the same way you feel, nor talk about my inner life the same way you talk about yours, nor will I ever be able to live up to your expectations that I will be the sensitive and caring male you had always dreamed of marrying."

Martha was shocked by Ralph's candidness, but for the first time in their marriage she heard him. She began to become painfully aware that she was trying too hard to mold him into the sensitive and caring person she had always desired. She then decided to back down on her demands and initiate a new effort instead to appreciate the good qualities that Ralph actually possessed. This, in turn, gave him the breathing space he needed to feel as though he could talk comfortably.

Ralph's outspoken message to Martha became a turning point in their relationship. Instead of making such hard demands on one another, they began to accept some fundamental differences between the two of them. Once the pressure to perform was relieved, their relationship improved significantly. It was now safe to be one's own self. It was now acceptable to experience emotions differently.

This lesson in acceptance is a good illustration of how friendship can begin to grow in a marriage. Indeed, the men are often oriented toward the practical side of life, but they do *feel* genuine feelings. Their early schooling in the art of remaining independent

has taught them to be slower at placing the relationships in their life in the same position of importance as
women. They are generally not as process-oriented.
Lillian B. Rubin, a social scientist, sheds some light on
the struggle men have with sharing their feelings.

> It isn't that a man can't name his feelings;
> he's usually quite capable of saying he's
> angry, scared, guilty, and so on. Rather it's
> that he's left with a certain handicap in com-
> municating words and feelings, experiences
> some difficulty in putting them together.
> Whether in a romantic relationship with a
> woman or in a friendship with a man, he can't
> easily describe and express the complexity of
> his internal emotional responses, can't readily
> talk comfortably about what they mean to
> him.[7]

It is our experience, however, that they can be
beautifully capable of entering into a meaningful
process when they are invited to relate to the challenges of a deepening friendship in ways that speak to
them. The moment of this realization can come in sur-
prising ways in a marriage, but when it does, it brings
with it a new richness.

Tom and Bridget had been married for thirty-five
years. They had been through it all: rearing children,
job changes, serious illness and a host of other realities
that are a part of marriages of such long duration.
Bridget was open about everything in her life and could
be read as easily as a short novel. She considered Tom
to be the strong male figure that she had always

dreamed about marrying. He was the practical, day-to-day, self-determining man who always seemed to be able to draw from a reservoir of strength that they both needed at times.

Life was moving along in a routine and undisturbed fashion until the day that Tom was diagnosed with a terminal illness. His physician informed him that he would be lucky if he lived longer than one year. When they heard the news, Tom and Bridget just sat quietly in the physician's office for a time and were very sullen as they let the sad news sink into their shaken awareness. For the first time in his life, Tom encountered a problem that he was not able to handle. The sullen atmosphere was broken only by Tom's crying.

Bridget did not know what to do, since she had always depended upon Tom's strength to sustain her. He remained depressed after the visit, then refused to talk. He repeated continually that he was devastated.

Several days later Bridget confronted him with the fact that he "needed to talk." She announced that it was time for her to pay him back with some of the strength she had gained from him during their thirty-five years together.

At first Tom was reluctant to be open about his severe doubts and uncertainty, but after some encouragement by Bridget to "just talk," he finally began to let go. He began to disclose to Bridget how frightened he really was. She even surprised herself about how beautifully loving and supportive she could be in the face of such drastic changes in their styles of relating. She found strengths she never knew she possessed. She continued to invite him to open up his inner life and share his fears with her. He did so willingly and they grew very close to one another over the most ambiguous but richest year of their entire marriage.

## Overfunctioning/Underfunctioning

It is important for women to understand that their husbands can be beautifully open and very feeling within their own unique processes, but not in the same way as a woman. A wife's task, as Bridget discovered, is to be inviting of deep sharing without taking total responsibility for all of the emotions in the relationship. In today's way of saying it, she needs to be careful not to overfunction by taking total responsibility for the emotional life of the marriage.

Many women have to work very hard not to offer their husbands suggestions about what they are feeling. Before Tom's illness changed the texture of their interaction, Bridget found herself offering Tom a "check list" for his feelings. Tom had to reach no more deeply into his reservoir of self-awareness than to the level of a simple "yes" or "no" to Bridget's incisive questions about his feelings. The "yes" or "no" came in response to her questions about whether he was feeling anxious, depressed or empty, sad, mad or glad, discouraged and angry, conciliatory or anticipatory.

Bridget's overfunctioning in the emotional area allowed Tom to drift through the adult life task of taking ownership for his own feelings and expressing them. His offering of a perfunctory "yes" or "no" was all he needed to do to relieve the pressure of the demands of interaction, then return to his practical life.

Women, however, are not the only ones who can be skilled at overfunctioning. The men can be equally adept at it, but often within the practical side of marriage. We often observe that men try to "fix things," giving themselves and their wives the impression that the complexities of relating can be repaired as easily as mending a pipe, cutting the grass or tuning up the family automobile.

Carroll and Marcia had been married for fifteen years. They were able to communicate quite well until it came to a discussion about the state of Marcia's job. She worked in a large office setting in which a demanding male supervisor made her life very complicated. After a long day of scrutiny under this supervisor, Marcia would come home in tears, and then try to explain to Carroll what it was like working under this kind of pressure. She confessed to him that she felt that she was either treated indifferently or criticized unfairly. There seemed to be no middle ground for her. Most of the descriptions about her work environment ended with her crying uncontrollably. Carroll, of course, felt quite helpless. The more Marcia cried, the more his anger at her supervisor intensified.

Carroll would then become visibly outraged, ranting and raving about how unfair the entire situation was for both of them. Several times Marcia had to restrain him from dialing the phone and calling her supervisor at his home in an effort to "straighten him out." Marcia would then cry even more intensely for fear of losing her job as Carroll attempted to fix her life.

One evening Marcia announced to Carroll that she was no longer going to talk to him about her work situation. When Carroll asked why, she stated that his animated responses were simply too painful for her to handle. She insisted that her supervisor was difficult enough to deal with, without having to deal with her husband's angry outbursts as well.

Carroll was hurt, feeling that Marcia no longer trusted him. Finally she helped him understand that he did not need to "fix" anything. She just needed to talk. Once he understood that Marcia's need was simply to talk and share her feelings, he felt more free and they talked more comfortably.

Marriages begin to mature as both partners give one another permission to simply be themselves, then discover the all-important middle ground of friendship, in which their respective strengths can be valued and affirmed. At the heart of this shift, like most of the major shifts in a growing friendship, lies the equally important task of learning to listen. Sam Keen, the creative and very contemporary commentator on the current state of affairs between men and women, offers this reflection on the mystery of the differences between the sexes.

> The question of gender is penultimately a problem, but ultimately a mystery. The social sciences can tell us how differently societies structure gender roles, how they define heroes and heroines, how they educate, condition, and initiate boys into the status of manhood and girls into the condition of womanhood. In this way we can strip away all the false mystification that surrounds gen-

der. But underneath the stereotypes lies a true mystery. God did not make persons— chairpersons, mailpersons, or spokespersons—only men and women. Peel away the layers of the social conditioning and there remains the prime fact of the duality of men and women.[8]

From our perspective, the capacity to listen and to dialogue is based largely upon an appreciation of the magic and mystery of some real differences between men and women. A reflective friendship is grounded upon the sense of awe, respect and wonder that these differences bring.

## Eye Contact

We have already said something about how men tend to shy away from eye contact in face-to-face dialogue. They prefer instead to talk while doing things: hiking, biking, walking or even working on household chores. At precisely the moment when a woman declares the enlivening energy of face-to-face dialogue deeply meaningful to her, her husband can feel the most restless. Eye contact, face-to-face exchanges, even physical closeness can stir up intense feelings of discomfort for a male. Again, we trace the origins of this restlessness to early developmental processes, where men learned to function more independently than women. For many men, the most pressing need during tender encounters is to resolve the tension created by too much intimacy.

Simone loved intense exchanges. She thrived on "getting into" people, and came away from every exchange with her friends with a viscerally felt increase of energy. Relating was like a "fix" for her. She was never more alive than when she could interact with deep feeling and genuine care. For that reason she was surrounded with a circle of close friends who were equally intense in their styles of relating.

Simone never felt the same energy with her husband. He was capable of closeness, but the intensity of their exchanges never reached the peak levels that she found so pleasurable with her other friends. She complained to him that he was "non-responsive," and pushed him to "get with it; get some passion in your conversation."

Walter generally felt bad about their exchanges. His experience told him that he was capable of close relationships but he also confessed to Simone one night that her style and intensity of relating made it very difficult for him to feel comfortable talking with her. He confessed that it simply overwhelmed him.

After much persuasion by Walter, Simone agreed to try a simple change in emphasis suggested by his therapist: to try walking and talking at the same time. This method would allow both of them to communicate as enthusiastically as possible without the discomfort of face-to-face exchanges for Walter.

Their first effort at walking and talking was so successful that they were able to talk for a lengthy period of time. They were also able to converse at a level that they had not achieved since their earliest years together. Simone could be her energized and spontaneous self but it was diffused for Walter through a constantly changing environment. Walter could reach for the right words, free from the wilting intensity of Simone's dark and expressive eyes.

The results they experienced enabled both of them to accept the method as refreshing and valuable. A year later, their relationship has improved immensely and they continue their practice of walking and talking each day.

As a woman, you can learn to be sensitive to the difficulties that men sometimes experience with sustained face-to-face contact. Accepting the differences in styles of communicating can actually help you fulfill your dreams that the man in your life will be open and honest about his feelings.

## Self-Sufficiency

Men generally learned to be self-sufficient during their developmental years and it heavily influences the ways that they relate to those around them. This gives most of them a position in their interpersonal lives where they are less wedded to the importance of approval from others. This visible sense of independence is often a source of frustration to the women in their lives because it gives them the appearance that they are "out of reach."

A woman can begin to understand, however, that the very qualities of independence and self-confidence that attracted her to her man in the first place are now an unnecessary source of division. Friendship to a male often means that his wife takes great interest in what he *does* as well as how he *feels*. A man likes to hear that his strengths add to the success a couple enjoys in their marriage. He sometimes feels hurt that his wife has no awareness about what he does in the course of a day, what his conflicts are, what stresses he is under, and how corrosive isolation can be in an all-male world.

A woman needs to know that the times of greatest pride for many males come when their wives affirm that they are "proud of them" for undergoing great adversity while managing to maintain their independence, autonomy and strength.

## Understanding the Practical

Some men deeply hunger to have their wives understand the technical side of their lives. They relate that they feel minimized because their wives will not take the time to understand what they do with their time and energy.

The men relate that they are expected to listen to all the difficulties their wives encounter with the workplace, rearing children and managing relationships, but believe they are not given equal time to talk about the stresses in their world. Some relate that they are even expected to be "too strong" at times.

They believe that what they do is important but find it discouraging when a wife shrugs her shoulders and declares that her husband's technical world is "just too complicated for me to understand."

Ann never really appreciated Jeff's independence very much. To her, he seemed that he was always pre-occupied with his job. She tried to engage him on an emotional level, but he didn't want to talk about his feelings. Ann knew that he was under great pressure at work and longed to help him in the worst way. Finally, Jeff agreed to talk one evening. He confessed that he had been so quiet because Ann had never taken the least bit of interest in what he does from day to day at his work. He even admitted that he was angry at her for her indifference and therefore kept his distance in order to punish her.

Ann, in turn, confessed that she wanted to get to his feelings so badly that she minimized what he did in his daily work. Once Ann understood how he was offended by her quick brush-off of his work, she began to take a genuine interest in what he did. She tried hard to understand the technical details of how he spent his days. Jeff, meanwhile, began to take delight in explaining to her what he did all day.

Once she began to understand how difficult his daily work was, she also understood more about his chronic feelings of discouragement. She found to her surprise that by focusing on the practical, he felt more free to talk about how his life and work were affecting him. His feelings now flowed more freely because he felt no pressure to talk about them.

## Reflections: Melding into a Spirituality of Friendship

Once again we suggest some practical ways to deepen your reflections on friendship with your husband. As in the last chapter, we gleaned these sugges-

tions from our conversations with couples and believe
that they can work for you.

1. Spend some time with your husband and
   invite him to describe his level of comfort with
   face-to-face contact. After doing so, invite him
   to dialogue with you and decide on some ways
   to deepen communication with him that are
   more comfortable.

2. Write down ten strengths you see in your husband that have helped you grow in freedom
   and strength. Now share these with him and
   let him know how much you appreciate him.

3. Take one interest that is vital for your husband
   and ask him to explain some aspect of the
   technical side of it. Ask him lots of questions.
   Ask him to help you understand the complexi-
   ty of it. Then see if you can develop a genuine
   interest in whatever it is he is explaining.

4. Ask your husband what he needs for adequate
   personal space in order to feel that he can be
   himself; then try to give him the support he
   needs to construct it.

5. Define for yourself how much and under what
   circumstances you need gratifying and dynamic friendships. Explain the importance of this
   to your husband and ask if you can work
   together to foster it.

6. Ask your husband if he ever "de-selfs" under
   pressure at work or in your marriage. Ask him
   if he would like to share with you the conflicts

in his life that take such a heavy toll on his emotions.

7. Ask your husband what is the most difficult aspect of family relationships for him. See if you can understand how he feels.

8. Ask your husband what is the deepest desire he has for improving your friendship. Share your deepest desires with him. Make a resolution about where you are going to change the ways you deal with one another.

9. Buy a gift for your husband that will help him enjoy the most practical and fun-filled part of his life. Present it to him with a wish that he enjoy it more.

10. Ask your husband what he values most about your friendship with him. Share what you value most about him.

## Some Notes About Men, Women and Agape

A genuine spirituality of friendship develops with hard work. However, we contend that unless the real differences between men and women are examined and talked about honestly, the efforts to build a genuine spirituality are likely to collapse. If a spirituality doesn't collapse completely, a couple can labor under the illusion that they are growing into a close union with one another and even with God, while at the same time never facing a deep alienation that exists in the marriage. The alienation flows from the fact that they have never heard one another at the level of real gender differences.

To find a sense of direction in this delicate and complicated matter, we refer again to the notion of agape. It invites couples to move toward the ideal of selfless love. This is an inherently difficult task. Some say it is impossible without the help of God. But under the gentle aegis of agape, spouses grow in friendship with God as they honestly struggle to be friends with one another. It is impossible to separate these two dimensions.

The gospel is clear: it offers an assurance that the God of friendship will be intimately involved with every effort to be loyal, every movement toward support, every question of trust, every laugh that is shared, every struggle at honesty. These deep movements of the heart lift spouses into the heart of God and bring with them a genuine transformation of the marriage.

# 5

# Transitions

*I've named you friends because I've let you in
on everything I've learned from the Father.*
*John 15:15*

---------------------❖---------------------

"We began with romance," she related as she tried
to recount the changes that had taken place over the
last twenty years. "I had done a lot of dating before
Dan and I met, and at first it was romantic and exciting
and all that. But the first couple of weeks after we met,
I felt so different. He was genuinely interested in everything that I did, and when we were together, we just
talked for the most part. It felt more like a friendship
than anything else. That is exactly what it started out
as and it just kept growing. No one really had to tell us
what to do, since we both had a good idea about how
friendships work. Now twenty years later, our friendship
has grown unbelievably. We still talk all the time and
we still continue to think of each other as best friends.

It has helped us get through a lot of years together; some of them real difficult."

Like the attraction of a warm October night under the harvest moon, success in friendship entices couples to extend themselves beyond the bare-bones dictionary definition of friendship as "a relationship of mutual affection and good will." Their creative interactions invite them to evolve into their own "special friendship," marked with their unique signature.

"There is something wonderful about the staying power of friendship," related one husband who was in a rare reflective mood one evening. His wife looked at him a bit suspiciously as he talked about their lives, probably wondering what shared secrets he was going to disclose to everyone present.

He continued unimpeded: "We certainly know a lot about each other's faults. By the end of the second year of marriage, they were out in the open. It is a good thing we emphasized friendship rather than romance to hold us together. The friendship business allowed us to deal with some real differences between the two of us. Actually, in times of great uncertainty, we worked toward a better friendship rather than an intense romance. It helped us deal with each other more realistically. We still have our differences ten years later and they can be difficult to live with, but we are still together, and we feel good about it." As he slowed his narrative, his wife breathed a sigh of relief that he had finished talking.

Most couples, if they have matured at all, relate that they are in an entirely different place (emotionally, psychologically, even spiritually) several years after their friendships first began. As the mists of romance lifted and the reality of their life together became apparent, they sorted out and incorporated into it a number of qualities that they equate with their very special friendship. These sustained them through deep changes.

Perhaps they were first bonded together with a strong emphasis on encouragement and support, as one partner completed an educational sequence. Once this phase of their life was completed, support was eclipsed by a resurgence of spontaneity, freedom and sharing, partially gained through the advantages of a good education.

Another couple might have been grounded in a solid sense of sharing and spontaneity, but find in their twentieth year of marriage that they are asked to draw from an untapped reservoir of support to help them through a serious illness in the family. As they drink from the reservoir of supportive love, they discover a dimension to their lives they never knew existed.

In all, the specific attributes which sustain a deep marital friendship and thereby undergird every transition in a couple's life are innumerable. Support, caring, honesty, love, communication, humor, sensitivity, loyalty, sexuality, sharing, appreciation, thoughtfulness, forgiveness, encouragement, cooperation, commitment and respect are often named by couples as critical for their lives. But so are respect, acceptance, openness, faithfulness, boundary-setting, generativity, generosity, compassion and closeness.

The endless litany of shared values and deeply felt virtues can go on indefinitely, each word describing an entire history, from its beginning in early marriage to a fruition in the shared maturity of later years: fidelity, closeness, understanding, a sense of presence, intimacy, interest, integrity, consideration, patience and on and on and on. Like a finely cut diamond, the many facets of friendship refract the sunlight in subtle yet brilliant ways, each facet highlighting, enhancing, accenting and giving rich color to the friendship itself.

Accurately describing the rainbow of colors that fill a room as the sunlight refracts through a precisely cut diamond is impossible. It is no less difficult to describe the rainbow of colors that is friendship. We will attempt, instead, to highlight six qualities of friendship we believe are most important in offering the continuity, depth and substance that sustain couples as they make the transition from early romance to a deep spirituality of friendship. We continue to hear about the importance of these attributes in our work with couples.

## Six Significant Qualities of Friendship

### *Support*

When we ask couples what support means to them, we usually hear a rich array of views in their responses, each one representing a deep dimension of caring that sustains them through times of significant change.

"He has always been there for me," she said. She appeared deeply moved as she began her litany of the many ways he had been so loyal to her. "I know him as a friend who accepts me now with all my weaknesses. He knows the worst and the best about me; he has seen me through graduate school and several career changes; he knows how fragile and unsure of myself I can be, but he is always there. Support is the best term I can think of, but it really doesn't capture the tremendous sense of loyalty that I feel from him. I don't know where I would be if it were not for his strength."

In this example, we observe the load-bearing structure of support and the way that it is so important in building a solid edifice of friendship. In this case, it sustained this wife through a long educational sequence. The deep belief of a husband in his wife's capacity to achieve contributed significantly to her new identity. Support in this case has a dimension of fidelity about it: he believed she was capable, and she discovered through his support just how capable she was.

Support often becomes integrated into an atmosphere of comfort and caring as couples meld gender differences into genuine strengths. "I always believed I was supposed to be the strong one," he recounted, "so I did my best to remain strong and resourceful during our earlier years. She seemed to gain from my strength, but I also found myself becoming more and more isolated, especially as our family grew larger. I really felt left out of so many things, since it seemed that all I did was earn more money in order to pay more bills. After a long period of not communicating I moved out for a time. This shook everyone up including me. When we finally began talking about what had happened to us, and I broke down and told her I was very tired of being so strong, she really listened to me. She acknowledged that she had felt isolated in her own way. This exchange became a moment of truth for both of us, so we pledged to begin our relationship all over again. The kind of friendship we had so many years ago began to come back to life, and we began to share more. Now we both carry the burdens of the marriage and support one another."

He looked relieved as he disclosed the final truth of the transition in his marriage which had freed him from his burdens, "Neither one of us has to be totally strong or totally weak." In their awakening, support took on a quality of empathy: they were able to hear each other's deep emptiness for the first time. This helped them work their way through a significant change in their tenth year of marriage. In doing so, they recaptured a spirit of friendship which they believed had been lost forever.

### *Honesty*

No friendship stays together for long if friends become dishonest with one another. This is true for casual friendships as well as marriage. Game-playing, double-dealing, deception, unexplained or unexpressed strains in the relationship soon make the interpersonal atmosphere too toxic to breathe.

Conversely, a friendship stays healthy because it is first, foremost and under all conditions, honest. Like the air of a cool autumn morning, it refreshes the senses and invites one to rejoice in being alive. Honesty can also have the sting of a cold winter wind about it. It can hurt.

We often tell couples in treatment that the deep honesty of a genuine friendship is a rare and precious gift that is central to building authentic intimacy. We caution them to guard it closely so that it doesn't slip away.

"I knew that there was a lot going on in the marriage that was not being talked about," she related. "We would avoid each other, often declaring that we were so busy with our respective careers that there was never enough time just to talk. The night he requested that we talk, I knew something was afoot, so I agreed to finally talk."

She hesitated to continue, biting her lower lip several times, then continued her story. "It started off quietly enough, but as he continued talking he got louder and louder about my avoiding him and how he felt so left out of my life." She continued, talking just a bit faster, "Then it was my turn, and I let him have it about his total insensitivity to my needs and his arrogance and closed-mindedness."

She stopped and reflected momentarily, then continued, "We stayed at it for most of the night, and were both too exhausted the next day to go to work. By then we had softened (or should I say worn down?). We were finally candid and honest with each other, and that was a turning point for us. We resolved to talk more often and never to be evasive with one another again. Now we are learning how well things work when we talk honestly, and we have done so much better in every respect."

As this couple discovered, honesty during a long night of disclosure awakened them to a deeper foundation for their friendship. It allowed them to speak clearly about their likes and dislikes, feelings and attitudes, enabling them to be themselves. We often hear couples equate honesty with the capacity to "be themselves in the relationship," and this in turn gives them permission to speak candidly about what they want from each other. This earth-shaking quality offers the context for many successful transitions from early romantic love to genuine agape.

### *Sharing*

Sharing speaks for itself: it is identified with the beauty and the challenge of life together in its many unique expressions. The broad applicability of sharing to almost any experience of intimacy gives it a universal appeal. This is the quality that most allows couples to identify themselves with one another in a common adventure of living.

"Sharing has changed a lot for us over the years," she related. "It used to mean a lot of fun together, and hours of just being together and talking. Then during the years that the children were growing up, it seems as though we had to work hard to find just five minutes to be alone and enjoy each other. We managed to preserve a time of sharing for ourselves, even when we were so busy with so many things. Now, it seems like only a few years later and the children are all gone. We're learning all over again what it means to share open time. We are fortunate enough to do a lot of traveling, and we talk all the time. It feels that we're coming back to the kind of friendship we began with."

For this couple, their transition to the later years of marriage is a gratifying one: recapturing the excitement they had at an early stage of friendship. They fought to keep their sharing alive during their child-rearing years, and it now enables them to build a fresh spontaneity upon that very foundation.

## Mutual Trust

Trust is nothing more than to invest faith in another person. Mutual trust is a shared faith in one another. It is a close companion to honesty. The contagious atmosphere of trust is breathed in, developed, nurtured and genuinely prized as an extraordinary gift. It brings with it a deep peace of mind.

It ages slowly, like fine wine, over a long period of time. For some, however, its aging can be laboriously slow before trust is finally integrated into the marriage in a satisfactory way.

"I learned a lot about trust," she began, "but I sure learned it the hard way. If I could do it over again, I would never have done what I did...but a passionate, misdirected moment." She hesitated, but needed to tell someone the rest of her story. "I slept with a good friend of ours and then my husband found out about it. It almost cost me my marriage, but after several all-night talks we dealt with the whole thing honestly. I can't believe he loves me that much to be so concerned about me." She hesitated again, then regained her composure. The tears began flowing as she continued: "I found out that trust is a very fragile quality in a relationship. We have a lot of rebuilding to do and we're going to do it."

As this couple discovered through a very difficult experience, trust forms a sometimes fragile yet indispensable foundation for marital friendship. When it is present, countless benefits flow from it. When it is absent, life together is lived tentatively, each response measured suspiciously, as spouses struggle to hold a fragile bond together.

### A Sense of Humor

Not all the qualities of friendship carry with them such notes of heavy responsibility. A sense of humor is one such trait, and we especially find this quality in the long-term marriages.

"There is only one way that we have made it through all these years together," she related. "We have been through so much change, have dealt with each other's craziness. We learned early in our marriage that some events are not worth crying over, that it's better to laugh about them. Our best times have been the ones where we have lightened up and seen the humor in our situation. The worst: the times when we took life far too seriously."

The deep pride manifested in her description of their shared life was quite obvious. She felt good about the success they had achieved during their long history together. "Even after twenty-nine years of marriage," she continued, "we are not without our conflicts, some of which are tiresomely repetitive, but we have learned to keep the fun alive. Friendship, faith and vitality are gifts for which we are humbly grateful."

### Mutual Respect

This quality also speaks for itself. As a friendship deepens, a respect for the beauty, honesty and integrity of a spouse deepens with it.

"We learned it mostly the hard way," he reiterated. "We are so different. We kept these differences in the forefront of our lives and badly hurt one another. But then we must have mellowed. We just decided to stop exaggerating the differences and try to respect one another. So far, so good. It is at least more peaceful. We now see the real differences as something that can actually benefit us both, and we also stay out of each other's way a lot more."

In this example, the transition through the acceptance of some very real differences and the movement toward deep union was grounded in mutual respect. Their capacity to see their differences as beneficial to the marriage came after much disagreement and a long period of reaching to achieve a successful balance between their strengths and differences. Mutual respect reminded them to set appropriate boundaries, communicate honestly and not control one another. In that way, their separate "I-ness" evolved and matured.

## Living Within the Context of Freedom

Couples who enjoy a mature friendship recount to us that their path has not been an easy one. It has been a journey filled with hard work, self-sacrifice and a continued struggle with their own dark side which keeps them from loving one another as they might desire. Unforgiveness has impeded their efforts at honesty. Anger has clouded their capacity to love openly. Doubts about their worthiness have pushed aside their partner's efforts to love them. Denial has kept them from examining their own flaws. Yet, their friendship has survived. It has patiently called each of them back home to the light they first saw in one another.

Those who arrive at a mature and deep friendship do so not only because they want it but because they are willing to do the hard work to achieve it. Freedom becomes real for them because they have liberated themselves from the oppression caused by unexamined gender differences. They find a shared strength in a friendship that is open, compassionate and honest. The call of agape continues to speak to them about the promise of freedom that comes from understanding what genuine love means.

A consciousness of God's presence in their shared handiwork seems to be unimportant for some. They are nevertheless enlightened and changed by the demanding process of living and loving. Sometimes the enlightenment comes during their darkest moments and deepest pain. Whether or not they arrive at a thoughtful and clearly articulated spirituality of marriage at this stage seems to matter little, for the rewards of hard work are sustaining to them and they enjoy the rich gift of friendship they have earned.

### Reflections: Transitions and Spirituality

We come now to the question, "How can a spirituality of friendship develop at a time of significant life transition?" In response to this question we suggest the following practical reflections on friendship:

### *Exercise 1*

1. Each of you find some private space in order to be alone for a time. Write out an inventory of the qualities that you believe have built the foun-

dation of your friendship. If you are at a loss about what to look for, we suggest you reread the first part of this chapter. Be sure to write out your inventory without consulting with one another.

2. Share the results of your inventories with each other and discuss where your similarities and differences are.

3. Now decide what qualities are going to underlie the next phase of your history together. Do you want to be more supportive and caring? Do you seek deeper honesty? Do you seek greater freedom and spontaneity? Do you long to develop a more compassionate heart? Select the qualities that fit with where you want to take your friendship from this moment on; then decide what you want from each other.

## Exercise 2

1. Each of you find some personal quiet space. Do some soul-searching and try to identify the one fault that represents your darkest side. How has this darkness impeded the growth of your friendship during your time together? What fears underlie the continued stubborn reappearance of your dark side in your marriage?

2. Take some time together and identify what the dark side is for each of you. Now draw upon the friendship you have already developed and decide what ways you are going to be supportive in order to deal with the dark side in each of you. Share what is your most sincere desire for

breaking out of the slavery caused by this dark side.

3. Make a plan of action for the next six months and decide in detail how you are going to work to deepen the friendship in your marriage. Include in your plan of action a weekly sharing to measure where you are with your progress.

### Exercise 3

Sit and talk for a time about a significant event that took place in your marriage (example: the birth of your first child, loss of employment, your children leaving home, a serious illness etc.). Share with one another what that event meant to each of you and what it means to you now.

What did you discover about yourselves as you transitioned through this event and arrived at a new chapter in your history? What qualities sustained you through the hard times? Have you retained any of them? Which one have you forgotten about?

Now discuss where you are with these same qualities of friendship. Do you need to revitalize them for your life right now? If so, make a plan of action that will begin to restore them to the proper place in your life.

# 6

# Deeper Truths

*You didn't choose me, remember; I chose you.*
*John 15:16*

———————————❖———————————

The hard work of developing a friendship can yield for a couple a genuinely satisfying relationship but it may or may not have anything to do with an awareness of God in their lives. The awakening to God can take place during any epoch of a couple's history and unfold in amazingly diverse ways. This represents a quantum leap in the way a couple begins to look at and live in a marriage. We note that a real deepening in the quality, substance and depth of marital spirituality takes place with them as they become aware that the destiny of their marriage is intimately connected to their relationship with God.

This leads them into a different kind of relationship, in which every bit of hard work they do to build a friendship is influenced, formed and deepened by the

presence of God. Recognizing and sharing the awareness of God's presence in all that they are gives a couple enormous reassurance and opens up a reservoir of
compassion, insightfulness and many other qualities
they never knew they possessed. In brief, they begin to
reflect the shared wisdom that is a reflection of the
presence of God in all things.

"I think it was that way from the beginning," she
said. He nodded in agreement as each of them spoke
in turn for the relationship. "We each grew up knowing
that we had a call to know and love God," he continued. "We met and our first discussion went on for
hours. It was about Thomas Merton and how we both
loved his writings. We read excerpts to one another on
the next date and felt really good about the deep sharing of our souls. When we married, we had Merton
readings at our wedding. We regularly go on retreats
together and continue to share the quest to make God
more central to our lives."

"It started for me when I lost my job," he elaborat-
ed. It was obviously difficult for him to describe what
had happened, since the memory of his unwanted
departure was so fresh. "I went from being an execu-
tive in a large corporation to an unemployed overly-
specialized fifty year old male whom no one would
hire. I was devastated. My wife was supportive and suggested that maybe we should look to God for some
help, since we could do nothing on our own. So we did.
We learned to pray. I was open to a complete re-evalua-
tion about the way I had lived my entire life. God
seemed to speak to us both about loving us, and our
lives changed for the better."

Both of these illustrations chronicle an awakening to God in the life of a couple. Even though their stories vary significantly, they do share common threads. The transition of a couple from a simple friendship constructed on their own terms to the deeper truths of a shared wisdom is generally arrived at through several distinct awarenesses. We now wish to explore these awarenesses in some detail.

## God Is Seen as Initiating a Relationship

"It began with me at a marriage encounter weekend," he stated. "I didn't want to go but finally conceded. As the stories unfolded about how these couples had discovered God in their lives simply by trying to love each other more, I began to see a pattern in the way our lives had progressed. My imagination was stimulated. I breathed a little more quickly. I got excited about our marriage again. I could feel a strong pull to want to know more, explore more and find God in our life. It really was the beginning of a new way of going about marriage."

Couples are often at a loss about how to describe their experience of the dawn of new life under God's initiative. In retrospect, the husband in the example above could reconstruct what happened but at the time it was not clearly understood. Nevertheless, as couples awaken together to a new sunrise they are clear in their conviction that God is calling them to a new day.

The God who was once shadow and a vague focus of love now becomes a real person. They recount that they encountered a personal God who spoke to them in a language that they understood. They feel called by name. They begin to open up their lives to the full implications of the call and explore new territory as the sun climbs higher, filling the landscape of their interaction with light and warmth. They slowly begin to realize that their future destiny as a couple is intimately tied to giving clearer form to the God of their new consciousness. They begin to believe in something greater than themselves.

## A Shared Sense of Destiny

"I prayed that I would find a wife who would help me become a good and loving person," he recounted to us. "When we met I had this strange feeling—that she was someone special. Prayer—yes, she is very generous and spirit-filled—keeps me on my toes." He recounted for us that this was the way that his marriage began. His awareness was that their destiny began before they met, since he prayed that God would be the matchmaker.

His wife of thirty-five years summarized her awareness of their marriage in this way: "God is love and our friendship is based on love of each other. We *feel* God with us in our daily living."

This couple speaks clearly and confidently of a shared sense of destiny that actually began before they met. They still interpret every event in their marriage as a reflection of the God who is their unseen friend. They call upon this friend to nurture, love, protect and form them. Their awareness continually deepens as they chart the course of their lives and explore the implications of their great gift of love. They anticipate the full entry into the heart of love which awaits them.

We consider the awareness of a destiny with God the critical awareness in the development of a spirituality. Once a couple develops it, they will never be the same. Every interaction from thereon becomes a bridge over which they cross into the warm and friendly domain of deep wisdom. Every effort to be a good friend, every event in their lives, every shared experience of growth, every prayer orients them toward the God of life and love. They begin to know that even the hard tasks of loving and the difficulties of life together are a reflection of the love of God for them.

## Love Moves Toward Agape

Couples are called upon to live their lives exactly as Jesus did: to explore the full implications of love in their lives and move toward its full expression of selfless love.

"I don't quite understand this whole thing," he stated. "I find myself resisting and resisting the difficult things about loving her, but I find a strength I never knew I had. She has been terribly ill for the last two years and I have had to let go of everything I had ever believed in about the joys of marriage, but I find my love for her has deepened. I seem to be able to ask God for strength when I need it, and it is there."

He recounted for us how much their lives had changed since the onset of his wife's serious illness. As he continued his recounting, he reflected upon how much peace and joy they had found in caring for and loving one another. He even registered surprise about how well he could do with these difficult tasks.

"We'll stay loyal to one another, even though we have no idea what we are going to be called upon to do. Our financial resources are depleted, so we'll have to learn to rely completely on God. We have never been more in love."

The awareness of being chosen by God to accompany one another through life literally haunts some couples. They find themselves drawn more and more into deep union. "We continue to be aware that God oversees our every action, every effort at loving," she said. "I didn't believe it very much at first, that God could care that much about me to give me such a rich marriage, but it has come clearer over twenty years."

Her husband joined her to describe his awakening: "She's right, you know; we are gifted. We know this God of love. We pray each day that God will transform our love for one another and, through it, touch others."

The shared awareness of a common destiny in a deep friendship called marriage is a reflection of the "yes" they speak each day. They *know* God has chosen them. They live and breathe their awareness and share a maturing insightfulness into the deep truths of life and love. It draws them ever more deeply into the divine friendship. They share the wisdom promised as a gift of agape: God's own wisdom. It is reflected in the realization that more profound truths hold this marriage together and give it life. They share that they are different now. Their values have changed. It is God who ultimately governs their lives and calls them to a shared destiny. Sam Keen reflects upon this reality of being grounded in the sacred as well as the sexual, in this fashion:

> The sexual and the sacred both shatter the categories of our understanding. After thirteen pages of careful reasoning of how we may give names to God, Thomas Aquinas concludes, "But finally we remain joined to him as one unknown." In the same way, man and woman are joined to each other as beings unknown, and we commune within a mystery that encompasses us. The love between us is a coming together and a going apart in which the fragments we are as sexual beings move together within the economy of an unseen whole.⁹

As the awakening to God runs its course, love itself takes on a different texture. Romantic love deepens into a mature commitment reflected in agape. The gentle influence of God's presence brings a couple to a more selfless love. Wisdom's gift is to know that real love reflects the unconditional love of God and they open themselves to it with all its implications, known and unknown. The need for distractions to fill up their lives is replaced with a simple kind of caring and sharing that bonds them together in uncluttered love. Deep loyalties and quiet conversation outweigh the need to be entertained. Time spent as a couple is reflected in an emerging gratitude in all that they are.

## The Self Is Transformed

The entry into the deep wisdom of agape invites a further transformation of the self. Here our understanding labors, for we are ultimately describing God's presence in a couple's life, and the work of the hidden God remains hidden.

"Our life just seems to be getting better and better, especially now that the children are all gone and we have a lot of time together," she repeated. "We are different persons now than when we first started. We are stronger, more caring, more real. I certainly have learned to be more secure and stand up for myself. I certainly know my own beliefs and my own desires."

Her husband continued to explicate their experiences of deep friendship, "I think that we are stronger individuals and that has helped us be closer as a couple and not get lost in the process somewhere. As we look back over our history, we can see that God has created our life with our help. It is beautiful."

The defined selves of the couple deepen through love. They become more sure of who they are and speak from that context. Their sexual selves are alive and well and active. This expressiveness with one another is respectful of some very real differences between the two of them. They have learned to appreciate these differences and blend them into a visible tenderness and care for one another that is contagious.

They have also learned to balance out their closeness with a capacity to express their individuality. These qualities of a healthy self are integrated into a comfortable balance, as it should be when good friends love one another. They work to keep their friendship finely tuned, by continuing to do the same hard work demanded in any dynamic friendship. They also call upon their friendship with God to sustain them through some uncertain times and move them ever more deeply into the wisdom that is God.

They move consistently toward an awareness that their true selves are grounded in God and that they are involved in a destiny that will open even richer gifts for their unique persons. In brief, they wholeheartedly follow the invitation to enter into the mystery of divine friendship.

The awareness of the living God becomes clearer with each confirmation of how rewarding selfless love can be: they know their deepest destiny (their real selves) is hidden in the mystery of the God of love.

They know who their individual selves are and they are adept at never de-selfing to gain each other's approval. There is no bland conformity in their interactions. They are alive in every respect. There is no forced reconciliation when they need it. Their interaction is textured with gentle efforts to get in touch with one another's real selves through open dialogue, honest encounters and rich, shared prayer. They live a life of openness, equality and tender caring.

"We could not have planned it any better," she said with a bright smile. "Let's give credit where credit is due. Our life has been the work of God and it has been a wonderfully fulfilling experience." "This is correct," said her husband, "The cycle is indeed a triangle, a continuous cycle blessed by our loving God. I couldn't have planned such a happy life that *he* has provided. God is indeed the planner in our life."

## Awakening to Deeper Truths

As the deeper truths of friendship begin to awaken for a couple, it necessitates that they develop a different approach to the development of a spirituality of friendship. Very simply, they learn to listen more attentively to the voice of God. This not only marks a deepening of their spirituality but provides the source for a different kind of reflectiveness in friendship. They move from less emphasis on the hard work of establishing the terms of a friendship to more of a shared experience of the presence of God in every dimension of their lives.

We believe that this call from God to live in deep friendship is universal. The image of Jesus at the Passover meal, initiating a call for all persons to come into deep friendship with God, forms the basis for our belief.

"We had done a great deal of searching for some depth to our lives," she related, "but we never really were able to find it." She chronicled the long journey they had taken in their ten years of marriage and the many roads they had traveled without having their thirst for God sated. "Even in our best moments together," she confessed, "there was still that emptiness, that longing, and we couldn't fill it up with each other's responses no matter how much we tried. It seems we spent most of our time trying to keep each other happy.

"So one day we were doing some reading and some reflecting," she continued. "It was a new book about a cosmic awareness or some such thing. We just came upon this idea: it was time to break out of the narrow confines of the way that we had been living and open ourselves to a higher power. I think something began to open up inside of each of us at that time: it was like an inner voice. It simply had a rightness about it. It fit with what we were looking for. We began exploring the great truths of the cosmos, seeking a higher power, and our lives have never really been the same."

The awakening for this couple was a significant step forward in their efforts to come into contact with a higher power. It eventually led them to a marital experience that spoke to them clearly about what they wanted for their lives.

We also converse with couples whose awakening signals for them a return to their own deep religious roots which have been forgotten "We had been out of organized religion for quite a time, mostly because we were so divided about it." he stated. "I was especially turned off by the guilt, negativity and oppressive structures that Catholicism had forced upon me as I was growing up. It was a terrible source of conflict for us because I refused to be oppressed any longer. My wife was hungry to reclaim her Catholic roots and get more involved in the church stuff."

His frustration over their entangled and seemingly unsolvable situation was clear as he told their story. "So we tried this and that but with no satisfaction. We stumbled around, attending this parish and that one, looking for some way to develop a spirituality that spoke to both of us. I guess all this time I was sifting through a lot of thoughts, doing a lot of reading, and I matured. I realized that most of what I learned about guilt belonged to another era. I discovered, in fact, that guilt had nothing to do with God, who calls us to freedom. There was no one person who clarified this for me; we just seemed to listen and respond to people who sought the same kind of freedom in their spirituality. Finally, I realized there is an enormous difference between a spirituality and organized religion. I also stopped putting so much faith in the clergy, realizing they were working out their destiny with God the same way I was. I guess I moved in some way from childhood anger to an adult spirituality. Now I find Catholicism has plenty of room in it for people like me, so I came back to my roots and I love them. That was ten years ago and we have been exploring a spirituality together ever since. Life is so much better."

God speaks to couples in a variety of ways: through the deep intuitions of life and love, crises in the course of a marriage, honest exchanges that bring them back to the deep truths about themselves and a multitude of other ways. We instruct couples to learn to listen to what their deep, inner voices are telling them. We ask them to make an effort to open themselves to an awakening that awaits them if they simply take the time and create the space that allows them to hear these experiences as the voice of God.

We offer, now, three meditations for helping you listen to the voice of God. If these meditations are helpful for opening up your lives, feel free to use them often. Also feel free to take some clues from them and construct some meditations of your own. In this way you can reflect often on the changes to your relationship that these meditations bring with them.

### Listening for the Call: An Individual Meditation

Take some time for yourself and block out all the normal distractions of your life. Take the phone off the hook. Turn off the radio or TV and begin to listen to the quiet. Set aside for the next thirty minutes all the chores that need to be taken care of and be prepared to quiet down.

Now seat yourself comfortably in a favorite chair near a window. Find a place where the sun is shining through. If it is not, find a warm and cozy corner and use your imagination. Let the warm sunshine begin to soothe your body. Breathe slowly, noting that as you exhale you are letting go of the burdens of life while your body is relaxing.

Imagine the warm sunshine as the love of God, who calls you by name and enfolds you in unconditional love. Breathe deeply and allow yourself to feel loved by God. Listen to the quiet within you. Repeat your own name slowly. Imagine God using your name and calling you into a deep relationship. Listen to the space within you and give yourself permission to feel loved. Do nothing more than breathe, as you listen to your experience. If you become distracted by unruly thoughts, repeat your name slowly and bring your awareness back to your inner space. Stay comfortable for twenty minutes.

When you have been refreshed by the warmth of the experience and are ready to go back to activity, see if you can carry the experience in your heart for the rest of the day.

### Listening to the Call: A Shared Meditation

Both of you sit in the same room but put a space between you. Seat yourselves where you feel most comfortable. Let each of you think of a moment in your relationship when you felt most deeply connected to one another. Breathe deeply. Be quiet in one another's presence for twenty minutes as you breathe your experience in and out, recalling to your awareness its significance. Stay relaxed as you savor it, allowing the experience to touch you and to remind you of how good your marriage has been at times.

Now come back into conversation with one another and describe to each other what your image was. Was it different? Was it the same for both of you? How do you hear the voice of God in this experience? How will you continue to hear the voice of God? What is it telling you about your future together? What is it telling you about deeper truths for your life? Who is God for you?

### Walking in Gratitude: A Shared Meditation

Take sixty minutes out of your busy life and find a peaceful place to walk. Perhaps the woods are filled with the colors of autumn or you have been blessed with a dusting of fresh snow. Lighten up and look for the beauty that is present in the moment.

Now begin your walk. Hold hands if you desire. Listen to the sounds of your surroundings and allow them to resonate within you. If the birds are singing, let your heart sing along with them. If it is quiet, allow yourselves to quiet down.

Take turns sharing what each of you is grateful for this day. Is it for being alive? The capacity to walk? The ability to see the blue sky or to hear the birds? Be grateful as you each share.

Now move to your marriage. Share with one another what you are most grateful for about your marriage. Is it the simple gift of being together at this moment? Is it for so many gifts that you have enjoyed? Your children? Their lives? Your capacity to make life a success? A vacation you are anticipating?

Discuss how you are hearing the voice of God at this moment. What is it telling you about your blessings and your future?

# 7

# Genuine Transformation

*I chose you, and put you in the world to bear fruit, fruit that won't spoil.*
*John 15:16*

---- ❖ ----

"God is with us and works through us," he stated with a confident look in his eyes. "We have a thirty-one year marriage behind us and we have grown spiritually together, and this has made our friendship greater."

He obviously took a great deal of pride as he spoke on behalf of their deep love for one another. "This realization about how much we have grown encourages hope in us. We used to live in fear. Hope has grown through love and caring for one another as well as spending more time together. We are optimistic about our future."

As we listened to him describe the ways that their friendship had matured through time and hard work, we could not help but be touched by their loyalty to one another. It was also clear that their love for one another did not exist solely for the two of them. It was the source of great good for others.

His wife amplified and articulated his theme of generativity as she continued. It was clear from the way that she talked that their spirituality governed everything about their lives. "A close relationship with God has helped me personally stay centered in our friendship. The Holy Spirit gives me the pull toward friendship. In the last few years our relationship with God has been pursued together and therefore our bond is strengthened—I think twice as much. The interplay of the Holy Spirit's grace with each of us individually and between us as a couple has literally caused a bonding, *enhanced* it, and that bonding in turn provides us with the ability to hopefully model that bonding and its advantages to those around us."

Their spirituality was expressed in a generativity that has opened up in ways that are beneficial not only for themselves but for many others. A deep sense of compassion for the suffering of others now colors their relationship with family and friends. They pray together. The transformation of their love into the spirit of agape described by Jesus has been apparent.

As a spirituality of friendship deepens it begins to reflect this quality of generativity. Love does not exist for its own sake. Love is inclusive in the sense that the security, peace and confidence that flow from loving freely invite the couple to open their love to others. It begins to reflect the love of the compassionate God who reaches out to all peoples. As the transformation of love deepens, we observe that couples reflect it in new awarenesses of the place of love in their lives. We suggest only a few of them in the following sections.

## Becoming Friends with God

There is a new knowledge of who God is, and this knowledge comes from God. Only God can give us knowledge of God, since our capacity to understand depends more upon the creator than upon our own efforts. Knowing God begins with the "yes" to the invitation of Jesus to live in friendship. It brings with it an intuitive knowledge of God that is personal and real. Sometimes couples describe it as a dark light. They begin to see with a clarity of intuition, and this intuition is brought to fullness through their efforts to love as Jesus instructed us.

"I first began to know God when my son was so ill," she began to relate. She was making an effort to describe an incident in which she had learned to listen to the voice of God in her life through a family crisis. "I prayed and prayed for his healing after that terrible automobile accident, but no miracle came. The endless visits in the ICU lasted for two weeks. I was really depressed, so I continued to pray for some answers about why this awful accident had happened, but there were none. It looked as if my son would be in for a long life of suffering after he got out of the hospital. I was angry, hurt, empty and terribly vulnerable."

She hesitated, then smiled as she began to unfold for us the experience that had changed her life. "When I finally let go and confessed my helplessness to God, things seemed to change within me. It just came to me: to learn to be compassionate to others since I had been hurting so badly over my son. There was also this reassurance that came from within: that my son would be all right. I had nothing to go on, but I knew it was God speaking to me. Tom began to get better later that day and eventually came through the whole mess with reasonably good health. The experience left an awareness in me of a God who really cares about us, even suffers with us. I just seem to be aware of this now at a really deep level, and it has taught me to feel for others who are hurting."

## A New Openness to the Call of God

A couple's transformation brings them to the place where they are much more comfortable with the presence of God in their lives. God becomes a loving and constant companion. The notion of becoming friends with God becomes so real that it permeates their awareness. It seems so natural after a time that they see nothing extraordinary in it. They speak easily and comfortably about it to others, while being careful not to evangelize.

"Where are we going with our life from here on?" she asked. She asked the question on their twentieth anniversary. They took a few days off to assess where they had been on their journey and where they might want to go from there. "To explore the hunger we feel for God," her husband answered, "provided you want to join me for the trip." He smiled when he said it, then waited for an answer. "You know I want to be with you," she said. "There's really nothing else to live for. I hunger for it and I want to join with you in your deepest desires to know God. All the business of life will fall into place after that."

This couple embodies what some of the great spiritual commentators have repeated quite often: that the hunger for God is more important than the possession. The knowledge of God flows more from surrender than from objective knowledge. It is always better to be open to the renewal God offers than to be sure of where you are.

## A Generativity Grounded in the Call of God

Jesus reminds us that we are called into friendship with God not just for our own sake, but to bear fruit that will last. We describe this as an adult generativity, and it reflects a rich array of ways in which couples implement it. "Since we share the same religion and beliefs, the common denominator of God in our lives has always been there and affects our lives together," she said. This wife of forty-one years was making an effort to describe the kind of generativity their marriage had brought to the family. "The celebration of our life together—the holidays, the baptisms, sacramental receptions, weddings and anniversaries—are all God-centered and are the frosting on the cake as far as our friendship is concerned." Her husband joined her in their shared expressions of love to their family, "Prayer is essential," he added, "and it can happen anywhere— home, church, on the street, spontaneously. God is welcome in our home and is trusted as a friend—with respect and courtesy. He is always there and is a good listener when called upon and often channels new perspectives and ideas into our thinking."

"Our children are all grown now and we are grandparents," she affirmed. "We have all kinds of time that we never had with each other, and so we can travel and enjoy leisure time." "We have a great time together," added her husband, "but we want to do more. We spend four months out of each year working for the SOME Program in the inner city of Washington, D.C. That gives us a chance to work with the poor and to reach out in some small way to give back to the world for the gifts we have been given."

This couple embodies in a practical way what Sam Keen expresses more poetically: that love generally expresses itself in a generativity.

> Love increases the mystery of the self and the other. In love we learn to love and respect and adore what is beyond understanding, grasping, or explanation. Strangers in the night, opposites joined in a passionate dance, keeping step to an echo of a distant harmony we must strain to hear. Moving toward and away from each other; two becoming one becoming two, ad infinitum.[10]

### Confidence in God

A genuine knowledge of God brings to the couple a confidence that their future rests in the security that comes from knowing the God of all goodness and life.

They possess a capacity to remain at peace even during difficult times. Peace sustains them and they enjoy being sustained.

God's presence in their lives reaches its most beautiful expression in their sexuality. They love each other deeply. Because they enjoy a deep union of souls and share the soul of the compassionate God, they are beautifully expressive to one another. The tenderness of their touch and the depth of their caring for one another has nurtured a blossoming of all the delicate and sensitive intricacies of their sexual personhood. Their lives become a transparent sign of the image of the creator as male and female.

## A Method of Meditating

The gap between the person and God cannot be bridged with objective knowledge. God is infinitely beyond our capacity to understand who God is. By issuing a call to deep friendship, God invites us into a knowledge of the heart. In other words, it is the heart that bridges the gap and forms the bonds of friendship between God and ourselves.

In an answer to the same question about how couples develop a spirituality of friendship, we offer some simple meditations on the largeness of this call from God. The meditations will help you learn to listen to the voice of God who speaks to you in a very personal way.

We see three steps that summarize the process of transformation into deep friendship with God:

1. acknowledging the darkness within each of you;
2. opening up to new friendship with God and your friend in marriage;
3. walking together in friendship for the future.

We offer the three following meditations as a practical way to open up the experience of deep friendship with God and with one another. Feel free to take the structure of the meditations and apply them to other themes as you become more familiar with the voice of God.

## Meditation 1
### Acknowledging the Darkness Within

Be alone for thirty minutes. Find a quiet space. Get rid of all the distractions of daily pressure. Sit in your favorite chair in the warm sunshine and allow it to touch you and warm your body. Breathe deeply as you allow yourself to feel comfortable. Find your center. Imagine the sunshine representing the love of God as it floods you with a feeling of warmth and healing.

Stay grounded in the love of God as you allow only one dark dimension within you to come into your awareness. Perhaps it is a tendency to control, to over-react to your spouse when under pressure, to be petty and narrow. This shadow of your darker self impedes your capacity to love.

Be honest with yourself. Have you acknowledged that this shadow is real? Are you still denying its reality even though you know it has caused unnecessary suffering in yourself and your partner? Imagine the ways that your denial has contributed to the unecessary suffering in yourself and your family. There is no reason to feel guilty about this shadow, but take this moment as an opportunity to accept it as a real part of yourself. Honesty is the beginning of healing, for God cannot heal what you will not admit to yourself.

Let the warm sunshine and the quietness of the space help you get in touch with the healing love of God. Breathe in and out as you allow God's love to touch the inner part of your person where you are ready to be healed. Be still and listen for the voice of God. Allow yourself to be healed.

Stay relaxed and comfortable, getting more deeply in touch with the presence of God in your life as the rest of the day unfolds.

### *Meditation 2*
### *Opening to New Friendship with God and Spouse*

Be alone. Find a quiet space again. Close out the distractions. Sit again in the warm sunshine and let it flood your person, coaxing you to relax and let go of the stresses, doubts and uncertainty of life.

This time, think of the warm sunshine as the unconditional love of God. It is unlimited. It gives life. It soothes deep wounds. It calls you to deep transformation of your lives. God loves you unconditionally. Jesus spoke from his awareness of this truth as the basis for his invitation to live in friendship with God.

Let this awareness sink in for a time. Allow yourself to try to imagine what unconditional love means. Ask God to embrace you and enfold you in the unconditional love he feels for you.

Now try to respond back to God with an affirmation of your gratefulness for this great gift of love. Ask

God to help you understand what it means to be God's friend.

Rest in the joy of God's love for a time and let it transform your awareness of who you are. Reflect on what it will mean in your ability to reach out to your beloved and other important persons in your life.

### Meditation 3
### A Shared Walk of Friendship

Invite your spouse to accompany you on a walk. Make sure you have an hour or so. Listen to the voice of your surroundings and reflect on what they are telling you about the beauty of today. Now share what it means to live in a deep friendship with one another. What is the most significant aspect of it? In what ways has it given you life? What doubts no longer exist for you about its place?

Listen to one another as you recount the ways that your friendship has grown. Hold hands and pray together. Get in touch with the loving God who walks with you. Ask God to be with you until your days together are finished.

# 8

# Nurturing a Spirituality of Friendship

*As fruit bearers, whatever you ask the Father*
*in relation to me, he gives to you.*
*John 15:16*

————————————— ❖ —————————————

Since our efforts in this book have been aimed at exploring a spirituality of friendship, we suggest that the best place to begin is by working to develop the best friendship you possibly can with your spouse.

If your spouse hungers for support, learn what it means to be a supportive friend. If you need honesty in order to move more deeply into a solid friendship, then make an effort to be honest with one another. If trust is what you desire with all your heart, then give your spouse every reason to trust you: in your actions, in your language and desires for the future. If you are encumbered by the burdens of life, learn to develop a sense of humor and lighten up. If you want your husband to share his inner self, take some risks of your own and share your dreams, innermost feelings and thoughts with him. If you want your wife to be affectionate with you, reach out to her in generosity and love. In brief, follow the rules for nurturing a friendship and you will find a spirituality taking root.

The very term *friendship* speaks clearly to couples who are seeking a richer life together. Even though the specific qualities which give the friendship form and definition vary immensely, the idea of friendship as a foundation for a marital spirituality is easily understood.

In our healing work with couples, for example, we have discovered a simple yet effective way to explore and open up the possibility of new life. We simply invite couples to stop treating a marriage like a marriage and begin to develop a friendship with one another.

Like an ancient sea bed, covered with layer upon layer of sediment, dead coral and past life forms, marriages become layered with their unique histories. When the word *marriage* is spoken, the sea bed shifts and heaves, clouding the waters with the sediment of memories, pains, past hurts and anxiety.

The simple substitution of the word *friendship* for marriage can change a couple's interpersonal geography from a layered sea bed to open space and clear-running mountain streams. "Let's look at your experiences differently," we suggest. "In fact, let's get rid of that overworked term *marriage*. Let's not think about reconstructing a marriage, but think instead about developing a friendship."

This simple shift in emphasis is often the beginning of a refreshing new view of relating. A couple's experiences almost automatically begin changing. Their intuition comes to life. It gives them clues about what to do during uncertain times. They begin making judgments about how to treat one another out of the reservoir of their past experiences of friendship rather than the obligations of marriage. When they are puzzled about what to do next in their life with one another, we simply ask them, "What would you do for a good friend under these same circumstances?" They usually know the answer.

From there on, our work evolves toward developing, enhancing and deepening the qualities of friendship. As the friendship deepens and they acknowledge that they are ready for a deeper spirituality, we invite them to open up their capacity to listen to the voice of God and to learn to pray together. When they begin to do so, the door swings open to reveal a landscape never before seen, and beyond the landscape they begin to know the God of all life and love.

### The Place of Prayer

Left entirely to their own resources, human beings are capable of only reaching a certain level of friendship, even if they work diligently to become the best of friends. Even the deepest sharing and the most intimate reflections on the meaning of friendship can be narrow and limited. To move toward the ideal of agape, couples must become acquainted with the sources of all life, love and friendship: the God of love.

This is the realm of prayer, and Jesus left a rich legacy for us concerning its place. In his instruction on the night of the Passover meal, he issued a promise: "...whatever you ask the Father in relation to me, he gives you." The message is very clear: the loving God desires to give us any gift we need to open up our lives, our spiritualities, our concern for others. All we need to do is ask for it.

The most common instruction we offer to couples who desire a deep and rich genuine spirituality of friendship is a simple one: "Pray for a spirituality and God will open the doors for you." We also suggest that it is best to pray for these gifts together, since in this way you will not only be asking for the same thing, but your very act of praying for a spirituality will bond you together.

"We never were very excited about praying together," she said, "because prayer for us represented too much of a formal effort. We grew up in a very traditional religion and never really realized there were a variety of ways to pray." She looked thoughtful as she told her story, then looked very pleased as she continued. "Someone invited us to one of those prayer workshops, so we both went in order to keep someone else happy, but it turned out to be good for us. We discovered that there are better ways to pray. We learned about prayer from the heart, tried it during the workshop, and then tried it at home, together. The lights just seemed to go on, and it opened up a new way to pray that is now very familiar to us."

She smiled as she continued: "We have learned to ask for things from the heart. We have also learned to appreciate one another more because it gives us a view of what the other person is thinking and feeling."

We also advise couples to be direct about the kind of spirituality they want. Jesus instructs us to be bold in our requests. "Very often," we instruct, "God cannot answer our prayers because they are not direct enough. If you want your love to be healed, make a direct request about where the healing needs to be done. If you want help in dealing with your darkness, ask for it. If you have trouble forgiving, ask God to give you the strength to forgive once again. If you want to know God more clearly, ask God for that great gift.

"Remember," we add, "you are not alone in this effort to love. God promises all the help you need to bring your love to fullness."

## The Necessity of Reconciliation

If you are to develop a solid marital spirituality, there is an absolute necessity for reconciliation. Marriage is too difficult and too complicated to go for long without the intrusion of some sort of offense, grievance, angry exchange or misunderstanding. We see these intrusions as a normal part of any marital life.

However, when offenses go unforgiven, they can easily move from the level of simple irritants to major obstacles in the development of love. They also cut us off from the love of God. We sometimes find couples who put their growth on hold twenty-five years ago because one or both of them refused to let go of a simple offense. A quarter of a century later, the unforgiven offense governs their lives. They never learned how to forgive.

"We went for long periods of time in our early history holding grudges," he said. "The tension around the house became so strained that it was really miserable. Neither one of us wanted to take the first steps to break the ice and heal the wounds. We shared misery more than anything else. Finally we decided to write out all the grievances we had against the other person on several sheets of paper and place them on the table between us. Then we would just pray silently that we could forgive one another. Then we would tear up the papers and throw the scraps away, promising to begin all over again with forgiveness. That began to help us. Over time we got to the place where we each began to take some risks to talk about our feelings, then begin to forgive out loud. We held each other to the agreement that we would forgive on a regular basis. It works."

## Putting On the Mind of Christ

The New Testament reminds us to "put on the mind of Christ." One translation states the mandate this way: "Do exactly as Jesus did with his life." St. John's gospel reminds us that we are invited into the life of God as we become friends with one another. To become friends with one another is to live out the example of the life of Jesus through our own efforts to love.

Again we suggest that this is the work of prayer, because we cannot do this solely through our own efforts. To love with the love of God is only possible with God's love.

"Marriage has to be the hardest thing I have ever done," he repeated to his wife. "Listen," she answered, "if it's hard for you it is just as hard for me. You aren't exactly a joy to live with at times, either. So why don't we both pray for the help that we need?" she pleaded with him. "We have been misleading ourselves that we have the strength and the smarts to do this kind of love by ourselves. Obviously, it is a lot more difficult than we ever imagined."

## The Root Command

"Remember the root command," reiterates Jesus. "Love one another." It is really as simple as that. The focus for all marital spiritualities, including a spirituality of friendship, is simply that of loving one another.

Couples often ask us the question, "Can we really discover God all that easily, just by loving one another?" "Yes," we answer them without reservation, "because to love a spouse is to respond to the deepest challenge of love. Marital friendship demands so much. In any other friendship, you can walk away when the demands of love become too strained. Marital friendship demands a constant and deep re-examination of self and you can't easily walk away from it. If you do walk away, it will still exact its price. You are confronted with the deepest questions of love and the worst kind of behavior, often at the same time. It is at once grounding and unnerving. Some of it is so big and so demanding that only God can see us through it at times. Yet even with all its eloquence and its triviality, marriage is the dwelling place of God."

## Nurturing a Spirituality of Friendship

We have argued in this book that a spirituality of friendship is the product of several factors which converge from different directions into a lived experience. They are: the hard work of developing and maintaining a friendship, a determination to move the friendship to high levels of maturity, an openness to viewing friendship as a gift from God, and a desire to journey into the heart of divine love. All of this implies an acceptance of agape as the foundation for married love.

The hard work of constructing the terms of a friendship can be undertaken with or without a relationship with God. The rules are the same for everyone. But to move beyond our limited human endeavors and journey into the mystery of agape is by that fact to open up a relationship with God. Very simply stated, we cannot achieve the fullness of a spirituality of friendship unless we allow God to befriend us.

Therefore, the first way to nurture a spirituality of friendship is to take the invitation of Jesus to love selflessly at face value. As we have seen, this can be a complex matter in a marriage, demanding a great deal of dialogue and understanding between spouses. It means much more than a simplistic kind of self-effacement that robs a friendship of every ounce of spontaneity and joy. As a friendship matures, the balance between a clear expressiveness of the developed self and the capacity to love another selflessly weaves into a rich tapestry of life.

We are also immersed in the mystery of divine friendship. It touches the marrow of our bones and joins the bodies of spouses in deep sexual responsiveness. It becomes ritualized as well in the many ways that couples express the meaning of deep friendship to one another. In view of these realities, we again offer some practical ways for couples to nurture their growing friendships.

### *Prayers for Couples*

Spend some time as a couple and find your private space. Close out all the distractions and be quiet for a time in each other's presence. Play a contemporary Gregorian chant CD at low volume in the background. The soothing chant, the themes reminiscent of sacred space, the atmosphere created by the ordered artistry of the music, and the connections with creation itself can create a prayerful mood.

Open the scriptures to John's gospel, chapter 15, verses 1-27. Decide who will begin. Read the text out loud very slowly and prayerfully. Each of you should listen for the voice of God in the reading. Then stop. Now reflect quietly on what the text is saying to you both.

Discuss the meaning of the text with each other. How does it apply to your marriage? How has God invited you by name into intimate friendship with each other? How has this allowed you to see the face of God in your life?

Now follow the mandate of Jesus to pray. One of you should take the risk and pray from your heart. We offer the following suggestions for prayer if you are stuck: ask God to speak to you more clearly about a direction for your lives. Ask God to open for you a deeper desire to love one another. Praise God for the many gifts that you have been given but fail to see at times. Pray for the on-going willingness to be transformed, especially in the areas where you are asked to let go of something to which you are you are attached. Pray for each other. Ask God to bless your beloved friend and bring him or her into deeper peace. Ask God to be a part of your day-to-day life: to guide, protect and nurture you as your journey continues.

Pray openly and with confidence, because you have the assurance that if you ask for anything that relates to an ever-deepening spirituality, God will grant it. Pray that you can learn to trust that God is working within you to bring your life to fullness.

### Write a Letter to Your Beloved

Take an hour and compose a letter to your beloved friend in your marriage. Spell out what this friendship means to you and how important it is for your life. Affirm to your spouse that you deeply desire to continue to share your life with him or her. Ask your spouse to continue to journey with you during the next phase of your life. Use your most descriptive language to extend this invitation.

Place the completed letter under your spouse's pillow or leave it in a special place where he or she will be sure to find it. Ask God to enlighten your spouse about the sacredness of your love as he or she reads it.

### A Special Gift of Love

Save a small amount of money from your discretionary funds. It would be better if the money you saved would come from a source whereby you would have to sacrifice something in order to save it. Perhaps you could forego a reward of your own.

Take the money and buy your spouse a gift that represents your special love for him or her. Include a card in the gift which you created or bought with much thoughtfulness. Make sure it describes to your beloved friend how important his or her friendship is to you. When the time is right, present your gift for no specific reason except to say that your spouse is a special friend and you desired to express that with a gift.

### Sharing a Special Meal Alone

Invite your spouse to a special meal with just you. Pick a place that allows you to share an experience of peaceful space: at home if it is quiet or a special place you both enjoy. You can even plan a weekend getaway, but make sure the place you choose brings with it a quality of quiet peacefulness.

Once you have found the place, slow down the momentum of life and begin to talk. Drink a few toasts to one another about what your friendship means. Drink a few toasts to your future together, then enjoy your meal. Think of it as nourishment for your life and food for your journey. You can even reflect upon the fact that it is an echo of the eucharistic meal Jesus shared with his friends.

### Sharing a Liturgy

Locate a place that maintains a reputation for good liturgical expression. It might even be your local parish. Select the place that speaks to you about God's love. Attend the liturgy together and participate in it as fully as you choose. Let it speak to you about the gracious God who invites us to friendship through this sacred meal. Spend some time afterward discussing the ways that this experience brought you back home to God's love and how the homecoming will influence your own deepening friendship.

### Viewing the Family Meal Differently

Meals. Meals. Meals. The routine of fixing a family meal is enough to drive a mother crazy at times, especially when there seems to be little thanks for the effort. When you have some quiet time, spend a few minutes thinking about how God chose a meal to speak to us of love.

Spend some time in prayer and ask God to help you find some ways to make the routine of cooking and serving meals more meaningful. Ask God to help you discover some ways that family mealtime might become a time of communication and love among all family members. The next time you serve a meal to your family, think about it as a gesture of God's love on behalf of your entire family. Think of yourself as an instrument of God's love. See if you can express the love that you feel in the way that you serve your family.

### Staying at Table When It Is Difficult

Jesus knew that he was about to be betrayed by one of his closest followers. John notes that "it was night" when Judas left the table to continue his work of betrayal. On the evening of their final meal together the tension among the followers of Jesus was enormous, yet he invited them all to share a meal with him and he stayed with them until the meal was completed.

Think of the tension in your marriage. What needs to be resolved between you and your spouse? Invite your spouse to a meal and to reflect upon the state of your friendship. Forgive each other where you need to forgive. Stay with the meal until you have rebonded, even though there might be big differences in your views. Let your spouse know that you still care.

### A Variation of Staying at Table

Think of the tension in your immediate family. You know that there are tensions, differences and difficulties among your children that are uncomfortable and nagging. Take a risk and invite them to your table. Be present to each one of them. During that time pray quietly that God will give you the energy and love to stay in a healing mode. Ask God to bless your every effort to bring your family closer together.

Think of the word *agape*. Jesus invites us to live out the ideal of agape in the same way that he did. Ask God to transform your efforts to love all the persons at your table in some new way. When everyone has left and you can breathe more easily, pray again that God will bless your efforts. Now be at peace with God.

### Feeding Your Souls

Invite your friend to take some time while you both just sit and talk. Ask your spouse if you can take responsibility for a few moments; then select a reading of some sort—a passage from scripture, a poem you both like, a new approach to living you found printed somewhere—and read it aloud. Ask your spouse to share the meaning of the passage, then just talk for a period of time about how it might apply to your life.

### Ritual of Reconciliation

The time has come to forget all the pettiness that can cloud a marriage and to ask your friend for reconciliation. Find your shared space, quiet down the surroundings, turn down the lights and be at peace. Light a candle and let it symbolize the presence of the light of Christ or the love of God in your lives.

Pray the Our Father together. Listen to the words that relate to forgiveness, especially the ones that invite God to forgive us in precisely the same way as we forgive others. Be quiet for a time and reflect on the ways that you have not forgiven each other. Ask God to help you find the openness to forgive one another once again, reminding yourselves that God forgives you so freely. Now declare your forgiveness of each other out loud and ask that God renew your friendship once again.

### Journaling

Spend some time alone, examining all the ways that you fall short of the ideal of agape. Do this not to feel guilty about yourself, but to develop a more honest view of how loving you really are. No doubt you will find a mixture of strong and weak points. Now write down the areas where you need to forgive more. Set a goal of taking one of these areas of forgiveness each week and letting go of it. Begin today with your first one. At the moment of letting go, write down how well you did.

## The Consuming Fire of Love

It was night again. It was also New Year's Eve and it was very cold. The snow began falling late in the afternoon, and by evening the wind was so fierce that a widespread ground blizzard was underway. It blew with such a fierceness that it created an illusion that the snow was suspended in the cold night air while the lonely highway drifted sideways. Driving was unnerving except where the road was sheltered by tall trees or high buildings.

Few cars were on the road that night, but a number of determined and loyal friends still managed to get together and celebrate once again the end of the old year and the beginning of the new.

"We discovered something new about ourselves the other night," related our hostess, looking very pleased with her discovery. The conversation took place in the middle of a crunch of people at the New Year's Eve party. The atmosphere was subdued yet cheerful as we all took grateful shelter from the brutally chilling winds of the night.

"We were decorating the Christmas tree a couple of weeks ago," she continued, "and there were just the two of us, Tom and me alone in this big house. With no kids around anymore, it gets awfully quiet, so after we finished decorating we just sat and talked. The only lighting in the room was from the Christmas tree and the fire in the fireplace. It was cozy and inviting, so we just sat and talked for the longest time. It was just beautiful—very quiet and warm. We hadn't done that for a long while. It was like going back to the days when we had all kinds of time to just talk and enjoy each other's company. We felt good about each other again."

This simple ritual of talking and sharing offers an excellent example of the mandate of Jesus: "Remember the root command: Love one another." It also captures the sometimes simple joys of a reflective spirituality and illustrates how easily friendship can creatively express itself in a successful marriage. The nurturing of a marital spirituality can be as simple as these spontaneous moments of being present to one another: just two good friends coming home to their relationship once again.

Sometimes, we two old married friends of twenty-plus years sit together and "just talk" in front of the fire on a winter evening. We reflect on what the root command means in our lives.

Our conversation turns to the topic of love, and to God, and how they interrelate; so we easily move to an image of the love of God described by John of the Cross, the sixteenth century Spanish poet and mystic. He described God's unconditional love as a consuming fire. John reflected that as the person (or the couple from our perspective) comes to know the deepening experience of God's love, it becomes a consuming fire and the fire transforms. John compared this process of transformation to the wood in a fireplace turning to bright flame as the fire consumes each log. Fire begets fire. It burns away within the person, cleansing every obstacle to selfless love, transforming every aspect of God's presence until the person takes on the nature of the fire of love itself.

The fire of God's love consumes slowly in a marriage. It begins with a spark of friendship at just the right moment in a personal history. Over time, the spark grows into a flame of love. It burns away through a thousand days of hard work and a thousand nights of talking in front of the fire and just being with one another sipping wine and recounting the fact that it really is *good* to be together.

Friendship lies at the core of our efforts to love, and it is through our living reflections on the gift of friendship that God most deeply touches us.

# Notes

❖

1. Sam Keen, *Fire in the Belly* (New York: Bantam Books, 1991), p. 222.

2. John Gray, Ph.D., *Men Are from Mars, Women Are from Venus* (New York: Harper Collins, 1991), p. 15.

3. Deborah Tannen, Ph.D., *You Just Don't Understand* (New York: Ballantine Books, 1990), p. 26.

4. Deborah Tannen, Ph.D., *That's Not What I Meant* (New York: Ballantine Books, 1986), p. 143.

5. Tannen, *You Just Don't Understand*, p. 279.

6. Aaron Kipnis, Ph.D. and Elizabeth Herron, M.A., *Gender War, Gender Peace* (New York: William Morrow and Company, Inc., 1994), p. 220.

7. Lillian B. Rubin, *Just Friends* (New York: Harper and Row, 1985), p. 98.

8. Keen, p. 218.

9. Ibid., p. 219.

10. Ibid., p. 220.